APPALACHIAN HERITAGE

VOL. 45, NO. 2
SPRING 2017

ESTABLISHED IN 1973

PUBLISHED QUARTERLY
by Berea College
CPO 2166
205 N. Main Street
Berea, KY, 40404

www.appalachianheritage.net

 Periodicals postage paid at Berea, Kentucky, and at additional mailing offices. ISSN# 03632318.

Electronic submissions only at www.appalachianheritage.net

Distributed by the University of North Carolina Press. Basic subscription price: $30/year for individuals, $60/year for institutions. For subscription requests and inquiries, visit the magazine's website, email uncpress_journals@unc.edu, or call 919.962.4201.

CONTENTS

INTERVIEW

CRAFT ESSAY

EDITOR'S NOTE

JASON HOWARD

Earlier this spring, we were invaded by squirrels—a gang of wily creatures that leapt their way to our gutter from a towering walnut tree. But their play didn't stop there. They found a small hole just beneath the overhang of the metal roof and enlarged it with their sharp little incisors. Soon they were running the length of the soffit, tumbling in their revelries on the vinyl sheeting, scratching on the insulation in the middle of the night.

It was pure hell. Our dogs, two little aging dachshunds, were irate. They would erupt in the dead of night, barking at the invaders and slinging their blankets with their teeth. We sat humane live traps for the squirrels, but often they managed to escape. We all lost sleep and patience, until finally, after using a combination of successful live traps and hiring carpenters to repair the hole, peace was restored. Despite the havoc and frustration wreaked by the squirrels, I came to sympathize with them, admiring their persistence in establishing a den of shelter and rest from the chilly March winds and April rainstorms, and evading our best-laid plans to capture them.

I long to be like these critters—inquisitive, fearless, resilient, determined to create a community tucked away from outside cares and worries. Literature can help to do just that, and in these times I'm reminded of the value of remaining curious and open, of reading to explore new worlds, while also using literature to disappear for a few hours from the tumultuous present.

I hope you will allow this issue of *Appalachian Heritage* to serve that function in your own lives. The stories in this issue will take you into the life of a mountain matriarch struggling with illness in T.M. Williams's lyrical "Murmuration" and to disputed property boundaries in Michael Gray's "Neighborly." You will be transported in the essays to a house near the railroad tracks in Rebecca Schamore's mournful "Trains," to a holler in West Virginia where a family is attempting to negotiate momentous change in Janet S. Holloway's "The Letters", to a university town in southeastern Ohio where the narrator finds a connection between transportation and national identity in Micah McCrary's "A Natural American." And then there are the poems—a moving quartet from William Kelley Woolfitt, a trio steeped in place and identity from Samantha Cole, and a paean to snake canes from Annie

Woodford, among other beautiful verse. Scott Honeycutt's insightful craft essay on renowned poet Charles Wright explores his Appalachian roots in East Tennessee, and Katherine Scott Crawford leads a revealing conversation with bestselling novelist Connie May Fowler about her new memoir *A Million Fragile Bones.*

While you read, as you nest, be like the dogged squirrel. Escape. ■

MURMURATION

T.M. WILLIAMS

She left a little at a time. The way the starlings do, lifting from a line off into nowhere, one by one until they're gone completely.

First was the index finger on her right hand. She was numb from sugar, so she didn't notice when it started to cook. That smell that mixed with the mustard greens told her. Like hog meat. And later the scent of gangrene, warm black rot, til the doctor took it down to the bottom knuckle.

"Maybe they can get you a fake one to put on it, Avalyn," her sister Connie had said, staring at the fat round piece. It was smooth and alert, like it might push through and grow itself again. "Wonder what they'd latch it on with?"

Her children banned her from cooking after that, said they didn't want her anywhere near a stove. Cooking was all she had. She told them that. She cried. And she argued with them and cussed them too, but the three banded together and were firm. It was sandwiches or whatever Bev, her oldest and her only girl, fed her from then on. Barbeque chips in a big plastic bowl. Ham and cheese on Bunny bread on a paper plate. A Hungry Man in its heat-warped black tray with mashed potatoes still cold in the middle. Sometimes some kind of candy Mamaw wanted but wasn't supposed to have that would push her reading over three hundred and get her all worked up thinking about blindness and needles in her unfeeling feet. Whatever it was would be set on top of her oxygen machine. It was the one her father had breathed on, lungs like two rotten apples from all the coal dust he ate.

When I came home in the summers I would visit her. We sat in the sun, her chimes going in the wind, our bodies held up by blue and pink fold-out chairs faded by light and rub. We looked out on the things that weren't there. The tree her husband had planted back when he was somebody she could love, cut down after it splintered in a storm. And the swimming pool that her son—my dad—had taken down after it sat empty two summers. Our chairs were on the lip of the deck, the wood reaching out in curved remembering. It was an easy way of being, an open-eyed meditation in the warmth near the edge with her there.

"You glad to be back home?" she said, and I said, "Yeah."

"You gonna make a doctor? Or you ain't decided yet?"

"No way. I'd work in the mines before I'd be a doctor or a lawyer," I said and smiled. It was a birthright to brave the bowels of the mountains, and I knew I could do it even if I never did.

"Your daddy might could get you on." She winked and turned her pink tumbler to her lips.

There were stories of women in the mines. The one I knew was of a woman who worked over at Rockhouse, the only female on the day shift. She took up with the bolt-machine man, who happened to be married to my cousin at the time. The men made crass jokes about the miner woman's calloused hands and the coal dust that caulked the lines in her skin.

Walking up the back road with her little collie dog on a string was Jan, who lived five houses down. She stopped and put her hand on the top of the chain fence. "Hidee, Ava! How you a-doin, honey?" Jan was almost sickly thin and tanning-bed brown. Mamaw waved with her right hand, but just as quick as she had raised it she pulled it back down to her lap.

She took up with the bolt-machine man, who happened to be married to my cousin at the time.

Seventy-five years with that finger, two months without. I forget. She told me this later that evening when we were grabbing a hold of the sticks of orange dreamsicles.

I watched her talk to Jan. Ms. Avalyn. You could tell she had been beautiful. Her face was kind and bright. She smiled and moved with the assuredness and ease earned from living through the things she had feared and waited for.

"That woman has had a time," she said after Jan was out of earshot. "Don't act like it, but she has. Last winter her husband shot hisself. She found him face down in the yard in his bathrobe. And they just the other day told her her daughter's eat up with cancer. The lungs, liver, cat, everwhere. She won't make it much longer."

That was the way with other people's grief. We held it out to each other for examination. We called attention to it like a passing curiosity of nature—a faint rainbow or falling star. It wasn't the same with our own. We swallowed it like laudanum, bitter sedative, addictive and dangerous.

■ ■ ■

Then it was her eyes. They were laurel green and clear like her mother's, like mine. There was power in them, I knew. I could feel it in the way people stared sometimes and sometimes changed their breathing.

Bev took her to the optometrist, and I went with them. Too much pressure, he said. Both eyes.

"Open angle glaucoma. After sixty it's not uncommon." The doctor explained that the medicine in the drops would increase the brown pigment in her iris, then he wrote her a prescription. She told him she didn't want it.

"Go brown-eyed or blind. Your pick," he said, and he patted her on the knee and left her in the white-walled room. The kind of room meant for bodies, not for people.

She cried the whole ride home. Bev couldn't coax her to stop. Neither could Elvis singing gospel or the redbuds moving through the window, frozen purple firework bursts against green mountains.

"Lord, Mommy," Bev said without taking her eyes off the road. "You're crying worse than Clara when she don't get her way." Clara nearly always got her way, partly because it was easier just to say yes to her, but also because she was Bev's only. And she was cute. Nearly everybody felt the need to point it out, and she soon learned that by virtue of that alone she could behave like a small tyrant. Bev said she would grow out of it—the tyranny and the cuteness.

"She'll hit her ugly phase around twelve. They all do. It'll humble her."

We pulled into the gravel driveway a little after noon. Bev got out and walked over to Mamaw's side. She was slumped up against the door staring into the side mirror.

"Walt wouldn't want me having brown eyes," Mamaw said. Walt had been her friend. I had seen her kissing him on the front porch years ago. He held her face in both his hands.

"Good thing he's in the ground," Bev said.

■ ■ ■

Her hair started falling out after her doctor put her on a new blood thinner. The last one had given her bad headaches and dizzy spells.

"Bird's nest," she said. She patted the spongy web twice and sank her palm into it. When she lifted her hand, the hair assumed its original shape. "They tease up what you've got left, big as it'll go. It's the best they can do with it, I guess. If it was up to me, I'd shave it bald."

"You wouldn't do it," Bev said. She was dusting the picture frames on the mantle and over our heads.

"I would too. One less thing for you to worry about. Wouldn't have to get me out ever month and pay thirty dollars."

"That is right. Hmm. We'll have to see about that, then. If we shave you bald and you keep your teeth out, you'd pass for Mr. Magoo."

"You'll think keep my teeth out when I kick yours in." She winked at me.

The pictures were of all of us. My dad with his black hair and bowtie. Bev squatting next to long-since-dead dogs she had loved. Clara in overhauls in a red wagon. And there were pictures of my mamaw's younger self, back before I had a name or a body. Back when the story ended with her, and beyond that were the syncing of a million miracles or oblivion—she couldn't have known. Her as a girl smiling next to her daddy, who was a cop at the time but would go into mining like his dad had done—like they all did. His name was painted white on a painted-gray brick wall, across from the old hospital on the other side of a ditch line. I had parked and walked and stretched to touch it.

"Mamaw, can I always sit in your lap?" Clara asked.

"Sure."

"Even when I'm sixteen?"

"Well, yeah, if you still want to."

■ ■ ■

Sugar took her leg. First it scaled over, pink serpentine discs, flaked and red. Then it started to purple, no longer a human thing, but a thick stalk of some poison reed. Then black. And the pills and the creams weren't working, so the doctor sawed it three inches above the knee.

She stopped talking. She slept through most of the day and sat straight up at night watching infomercials spit squares of light against the bedroom wall. The sweatered men and coiffed women with their white-toothed enthusiasm for small appliances or cleaning agents, which, even if persuaded, she couldn't afford.

"I bet I've lost a good thirty pound or better," she told Connie, once she started feeling better and would let people come visit. Connie sat next to Mamaw on the bed and sometimes touched her shoulder or took her hand and patted it.

"Wonder what they did with it?"

"Who knows."

"You think they threw it out? Or maybe they're keeping it pickled in a big jar."

"I hope they gave it to those medical kids to poke around on. At least it'd do somebody good."

Connie had brought her lunch from Dairy Queen. Mamaw liked the gravy they put in the chicken strip meal. "It's hard to get good store-bought, but this ain't too bad."

When Connie left, I stayed sitting in Mamaw's wheelchair beside her bed. I looked down at her leg. There was no sign of violent separation, just a soft, round loaf tucked into itself in the middle. Sometimes I thought I saw it jerk.

"Does it hurt?"

She looked at the TV and then back at me in a way that made me brace for something I didn't want to hear.

"Not really. My toes still itch, though." She looked down at where they would've been. "Itch so bad I want to scratch 'em til they bleed."

She looked at the TV and then back at me in a way that made me brace for something I didn't want to hear. Something that would cut through the comforting lull of the television and the clicking ceiling fan, maybe drop the word death between us so that we both had to look at it together. But she just asked me if I thought Wal-Mart would let her buy one shoe instead of a pair. Then she smiled at me, but I wasn't sure if she was joking.

Sometimes I wondered what she did to earn it all. Maybe there was some still-secret sin that brought it on and her punishment fit a crime I didn't know about. There had to be something. I didn't want God to be some machine at the

Chevron spitting out scratch offs, everybody's ticket curled and hanging like a tongue.

"You want ham or roast beef?" Bev hollered from the kitchen.

"Don't matter."

"What?"

"It don't matter!"

When I walked into the kitchen, Bev was dancing Mamaw's dog Daisy around like she was an agitated baby. She sat her down, and Daisy jetted off toward the front room to clamber under Mamaw til she picked her up. Bev untwisted the plastic on the loaf that lived on top of the microwave.

"Roast beef it is."

I was leaning against the candy drawer, where Mamaw kept Almond Joys and Little Debbies for the grandkids to eat on, when Clara walked into the kitchen pushing on the iPad Bev had bought her for Christmas.

"When Mamaw dies, I get Barbies. Ain't that right, Mom?"

Clara's fat face was flushed and beaming. She coveted Mamaw's Barbie collection, would stare at them on their shelves and touch the plastic front of their boxes.

"Is that right?" I said.

"Yep. Ain't it, Mom?"

"Hmm." Bev put a finger to the side of her mouth like she was really thinking. "Well, now, I don't believe so. Mamaw told me that when she dies, they're gonna put you down in that hole with her. Stand you right up on the box and pile dirt on your head." She said it straight, like she was telling the time.

"No," Clara said, but she wasn't sure. When you're six every story gets a chance.

"Mamaw said she loves you so good that she wants you right with her. The Barbies have to stay up here with me."

Clara balled up a fist and jumped on Bev's sock feet twice, hard as she could, then ran out the back door.

"Last week," Bev said. She never had a segue. All her stories were just sitting in a queue waiting to get told. "Last week she tried to wash clothes by herself. She knew I was gonna take care of it, but you know how she does. She held on to the washing machine and stood herself up and started loading clothes from the hamper basket. She looked so good standing there," she said. She looked away from me and toward the window. "I hate it so bad."

■ ■ ■

The last part was the hardest, when her mind left before her body would. Her eyes were bugged and angry. She was always suspicious, always willing an argument nobody wanted.

"Get her offa me," she told Bev, and pushed Clara, who was hugging her with one arm and trying to show her a game on the iPad.

"She's gonna leave," Bev said, "and I won't have nobody when she does."

She never got better. Bev called hospice. The morphine softened everything and let her let go.

I don't remember her. I recollect her. *Re-collect.* I cobble together the bits I can conjure and try to make her whole again. They don't always come together like I want them to. They're often scattered pieces, faded and anchored to the ground of my mind. But sometimes when I'm half dreaming, all the things that made her pool together and rise up, form a loose cloud of memory, twisting and dancing through the nothing between earth and sky. And for a moment I can see her as she was—whole and beautiful and moving easy toward the ether. ■

GLASSWORKS HOT ROOM AS PENTECOSTAL CHURCH

Wheeling, West Virginia

In the hot room,
while the finishing men
shape glass with pucellas
and shears, the snapper boy

tongs the gathers—jars,
jugs, flasks, and bottles—
into the glory hole,
that they may reheat,

soften, be carried by him
to the sweat-slick finishers,
their necks and lips to be
flared and grooved. He stares

into the glory-flames, dizzies
and cries out: there's a hot
room in the flames, smaller
than his, but brighter, molten,

wavering, the finishers singing
to the glass, and a bent boy
with tongs, reaching for him
as he sways.

WILLIAM KELLEY WOOLFITT

ANOTHER SIGHTING

Mercers Bottom, West Virginia

When he sees a shadow veer
in the sky, when my TV squeaks
and whirs, when we can't sleep,
we blame a bird-thing, a moth-man,
a mutant crane said to have risen
from the wooded area near
the boarded-up dynamite plant
on Potters Creek Road.
A lot of waste ponds out there,
he tells me. *Unlined pits, the army's*
chemical dumps. He points his finger
at me and grins. *I could shoot it,*
he says. I'm tired of him, of this.
If the crane looks into the pond—
filmy, swirling with poisons—
it must see a murky reflection,
at best, a stranger it barely knows.
In the morning, the toast burns.
I cry out *soul my soul,* drowse
at breakfast, go to the sink
and wash my eyes.

WILLIAM KELLEY WOOLFITT

DIRTY POWER

We are being forced to bear the burden of dirty power for Nevada. –William Anderson, chairman of the Moapa Band of Paiutes

near the generating station

Coal ash they breathe, coal ash
they take in, coal ash in the water,
in the air, bottom ash, fly ash,

boiler slag, from the residue ponds,
from the too-full pits. Coal ash
comes when the wind blows wrong,

coal ash hazes over the travel plaza,
glooms the fireworks tent, coal ash
on the block houses, the children

sculpting an eagle float from wire,
from tissue paper that the wind rips
and smears. Someone prays

for the turbines to be torn down,
the smokestacks brought low,
yuccas replanted, beavertail

and cholla fruiting after rain.
Someone sees a field agleam,
glass squares tilted for the gathering

of sun, the harvest of heat.

WILLIAM KELLEY WOOLFITT

PIÑON TIME

And he walks all day with his family,
up into the hills, for it is the time after
the agave hearts and screwbeans,
before the rabbit drive. And they camp
in the piñon groves. His boy looks for
kindling while he chooses a ready tree.
With a hooked pole, he grabs a limb,
shakes and shakes as gold needles
fall on his girls, as cone scales,
bark-bits, and resin-flecks land
on their arms, faces, and hair.
And they catch the cones in aprons,
in burlap. And while his boy digs up
the hulling stones, his wife makes fire,
cracks the cones, and browns the nuts
in a willow tray of coals she turns
and turns. And they sleep in a wickiup
of branches tied with yucca rope.
And if a glittering lizard swallows
all their nuts while they dream,
he will track the lizard, cut it open,
and take back the nuts, if squirrels,
if thieves—for it is the time
of green cones, and pine smoke,
his family working under the trees,
the brush of needles, coals sputtering,
and the crack of flame.

WILLIAM KELLEY WOOLFITT

TRAINS

REBECCA SCHAMORE

Up the steep wooded hill behind my house in northeastern Tennessee lies an open field that has always reminded me of Bambi's meadow. I often wonder, as I watch them pass through, if the deer that traverse our woods stop at its edge and counsel their fawns on the danger lurking in that wide sunny spot. They forage here regularly on their way down from the mountain that is the focal point of my Appalachian town. On the far side of the meadow behind a rusting chain link fence, railroad tracks wend westward through the neighborhood on their way to Kentucky coalfields. The tracks are generally quiet, but sometimes at dusk as the chickadees and titmice softly chatter in their hushed evening tones, and the last light dances through the summer leaves, I catch the rolling rumble through the trees, and I remember the trains of my childhood.

I was still a child, five or six, when my grandmother first played her train records for me. I was mesmerized by the soulful complaint of the instrumental "Train Blues," but I was too young to manipulate her high fidelity phonograph by myself. I had to ask Grandma to set the needle on the records and turn them over to hear the other side. Because I loved to dance and pretend and because I was shy and self-conscious, I would only ask her to play the records when my sister and cousins were outside playing. All alone, I would spin around the room, a whirling dervish, as the train thundered down the track, then collapse in a heap at the sadness in the fiddle's lonesome song.

The trains of my childhood were mythic trains, trains of story and trains of song. The 1954 edition of Watty Piper's *The Little Engine That Could* with its bright orange cover and its little blue engine spoke to me of kindness and optimism. I could not forgive the passenger and freight engines their haughty cruelty at leaving the toys and the broken-down train behind, nor could I understand the tired old engine's unwillingness to try.

I adored the Little Blue Engine for pulling that broken train over the mountain and for helping deliver the toy animals and dolls, the *picture* puzzles, the *big golden oranges*, and the *red-cheeked apples* to the waiting boys and girls. That over the top moral lesson was not lost on five-year-old me. The Little Blue Engine was kind and helpful, she personified my kindergartner's belief in who we should be. Best of all, she thought she could, and she did.

If *The Little Engine that Could* was my song of innocence, my grandmother's records—those train ballads of Woody Guthrie, Cisco Houston, the Weavers, and so many others—were my songs of experience. I didn't need to understand the songs; it didn't matter. I knew enough, that there were trains, mines, and hardship. I knew that tarriers, whatever they were, had to "work all day for the sugar in [their] tay." And I knew, because Tennessee Ernie Ford told me, that you could "load sixteen tons" but all you'd get is "another day older and deeper in debt."

The story that spoke most clearly to my younger self's sensitivity was "The Ballad of Casey Jones." All the other songs were simply a prelude. I acted out the story in my grandmother's living room. I wanted to warn Casey; I cried every time he said goodbye to his wife and climbed on that fateful train. I would stand in the great green chair by my grandmother's picture window and stare down imaginary tracks until I could see the train blocking Casey's path. I spent hours dancing and singing in that sunny room. If my grandmother or grandfather happened by and glanced my way, I would sit down so fast that sometimes I sent their oversized green footstool skidding across the floor. My play was private. I rode the Wabash Cannonball, took the night train to Memphis, and mourned the loss of that "brave engineer," Casey Jones, all by myself.

After my grandfather died, my sisters and cousins and I took turns staying with my grandmother. We loved those nights when we got to stay by ourselves. Grandma would put two little green Coke bottles in the freezer and if we waited long enough we could have frozen Cokes and popcorn that Grandma popped in a pan on the stove. If the drinks froze solid, we had to wait for the slush to melt so it wouldn't rise up and overflow the bottle. I would inevitably jab my straw in the bottle to suck down my drink, and the syrup would spill down the side leaving me with a half-filled bottle of tasteless slush and ice. Though it was better to wait and let the Coke thaw to just the right temperature, I was never patient enough.

One warm summer evening, I stood in the front yard watering my grandmother's ivy and waving goodbye to my parents. Distracted, I didn't notice the water spilling out of the ivy bed onto the sidewalk. Suddenly my feet began to tickle. I looked down to see an army of granddaddy long legs washing out of the banks of the ivy bed, frantically trying to escape the flood by climbing up my bare legs. I dropped the hose and started screaming never thinking to get out of the way. As the ivy and sidewalk kept flooding, the spidery creatures kept marching their spidery long legs out of the gushing water, up my goose-bumped skin. I stood transfixed by terror and kept right on screaming.

I rode the Wabash Cannonball, took the night train to Memphis, and mourned the loss of that "brave engineer," Casey Jones, all by myself.

At last my grandmother rushed out of the house to rescue me.

That night she let me sleep in her bed, but it wasn't long before I woke up screaming again, slapping at my twitching legs. Grandma turned on the light. Finally, to distract me, she pulled a big tin of pictures from the trunk at the end of her bed and began to show me pictures of my mother and her siblings when they were little. We came to a picture of a man I didn't recognize; his upper lip was contorted and scarred. "Who is that?" I asked. "He is scary."

My grandmother told me the man in the picture was my grandfather's father, and that he had been born with a cleft lip. He was a nice man, she said. He had lived with them for a while. I was stuck on that cleft lip, I did not know what that was, but to my childish eyes his appearance was frightening.

"Where is he now?" I asked, still wary of him.

"He died," she said. "He was hit by a train."

"Good!" I interrupted, and then almost as immediately gasped at the horrible thing I had just said.

I couldn't unsay those words; I tried. "I am not glad he was hit by a train," I offered. But I still felt relief that the scary man was gone. My grandmother laughed off my embarrassed discomfort. He did look a little scary, she agreed.

I forgot about the granddaddy long legs. I wanted to ask about that accident but was too shy to pursue my curiosity. I thought of the times my grandfather had wandered past the living room and stopped to watch as I acted out the same familiar ballads. I had played and danced and sung to those records never knowing the story of his own father's terrible death. That night I fell back asleep to the mournful rumble of a faraway train.

■ ■ ■

I continued to wonder about the accident that killed my great-grandfather. Before she died, my aunt told me the story. In 1943, she was thirteen years old. Her grandfather was a widower who had been living temporarily with his son's family in Louisville, so he could ride with some other workers to a plant in Indiana to work at a munitions factory. The night of the accident the men were driving back late in what my aunt called a panel truck. Several workers, my great-grandfather among them, were sitting in the back of the truck as it approached the railroad tracks. There was no light and no crossing gate. The driver of the truck never saw the train coming. My great-grandfather and two other men were thrown from the back of the truck and killed.

■ ■ ■

When I was nineteen and a student in college, my grandmother gave me her collection of train records. "You loved them better than anybody," she said. And I did.

■ ■ ■

It is late and I am standing outside in the driveway calling my dog on one of the last days of summer. At first I am so intent on peering into the dark for the light of her coat that I don't hear the muffled backdrop to the tree frogs and other night noises. Just as I cock my head to listen, the train blows several short blasts, and I know exactly where it is, a troublesome blind crossing over a dangerous turn in the road a few miles away. Ten years ago there were no gates or light there; tonight, I hope, the tracks are safe.

Tonight I remember my grandfather and the father he lost on a dark night. I remember other trains, their haunting ballads of loss and hope. In the afternoon when I am busy in the garden, or inattentive, the whistle's blow melts into the sounds of the day, a lonesome backdrop I never hear.

Tonight, Peter, Paul, and Mary echo in my head, and the whistle takes me back to the house that is the bedrock of my childhood memories. I am a little girl staring out the big picture window over the backyard, down the steep hill, into the woods beyond. The record is playing a train song, and I can hear the whistle blow a hundred miles. ■

LOVE OF THE WORD

As time went by, he marked
that grueling place in his heart
as one he loved. A love of the word, even
tipple.
With the smoke and blazing light, the hearth
where trains came to load up again,
to be completely filled,
rattling with noise and dirt, this tipple.
Down the road, Hurricane Gap, further
up the line, Jackson.
And his place, above it all, the little freezing
metal shack.
Overseeing the machinery
that moved like hands waving, transporting
ton after ton of the black and hardened
earth, compounded by eons of heat and pressure.
Now to bring heat to furnaces
and stoves. A beautiful
thing, this tipple.
Once, he heard someone
use the world he loved the other way,
meaning
just a little drink, and he laughed
as he set his empty glass
back on the bar, and headed
for bed at home.

SAMANTHA COLE

WITH NOTHING OR NO ONE IN BETWEEN

I heard him use the word, *directly,*
and I knew he was cut from the righteous
cloth. Knew he was of the promised
land, folded and refolded onto itself
to create mountains and ridges and hollers.
Precious cloth that stood,
like a baptismal gown,
ruffled by a hand
larger than any human.
And I say, directly, brother,
it is not how you say the word,
but the word you are saying...
directly,
formed with a slight lilt.
A rolling of your tongue
that makes me believe
you would be good at kissing
in the backseat of a truck,
and probably even better
at fixing it, directly.

SAMANTHA COLE

LESSON IN WEARING HEELS, 1994

Take measured steps.
Don't jut out your hips
or swing them too much.
You will look like a giraffe,
or, worse,
a whore.
Keep your chest up.
Unsure steps taken across
a slick tile floor.
First pair of heels after five years
circulating the sun.
Stick tread on the bottom
so you do not slide
and tumble
and your slip come peeking
out from beneath your skirt.
Heaven forbid.
Back straight.
Don't look at your feet, honey,
they'll think you are crazy.
Walk like a grown woman.
Stuff the toes with Kleenex,
make them stay in place,
wear a Band-Aid on your heel,
try to keep the blisters from bubbling up under skin.
Sometimes, playing
the "fairer sex,"
is anything but fair.

SAMANTHA COLE

NEIGHBORLY

MICHAEL GRAY

A Saturday in autumn, early and quiet. It started simple like that. If it'd been one of her boys I would've laughed myself dead, but with Ruth in mind the whole thing seemed more serious somehow. Maybe cause we all knew her so well. We could imagine her coming out for the paper in that plump blue robe of hers, hardly awake, white hair still mussed from the pillows. Then not three steps out the front door, her bare toes brushing against something setting beside the porch rail, something with heft. Said it took her a whole minute before she realized what was laying there, staring right back at her.

Half-hour after that I was easing my cruiser along the single-lane mountain roads, still about three coffees shy of living. I turned left off Gambill onto Locust Drive and followed it all the way up. Only five homes at the end of Locust, all of them tucked in thickets set back from the road. Few of those properties butt up against the pastures of the old Nance Farm. It can be pretty country to look at.

There's a NO OUTLET sign just in sight of the first two houses. I stopped the car there, picked up the handset to see if Joe was still listening.

From the other end, he asked, "How's it look?"

I stared out the windshield. "Got the whole damned Pelfrey clan up in Farler's driveway this time."

"What're they up to?"

"Well...looks like they're just carrying on at the moment."

"Need one of us to come out?"

"That's okay, I'm already here." I thought it over, still staring. "Keep the radio close though, huh?"

Joe said, "Have at 'em."

■ ■ ■

To look at the big ole brick split-level, you might not expect the owner to be someone as small and brittle as Ruth Pelfrey. Fifty-plus years in the same house, same big yard with the one side sloping down to the creek.

Same neighbors too except for the Farlers, who'd moved into the cottage across the street not three years earlier—

Henry and Tarah and their twin girls. Nice little group far as I could tell, and they got along with Ruth fine, but just the same it didn't take long for trouble to start.

No mystery why either. Mitch, Ellis, and Danny—Ruth's three boys.

They're the one feature about the old girl a lot of people can't abide. Before the two eldest even reached their teens, it got to where you couldn't help separating them in your mind, almost like you were preserving something about their momma by doing so. Ruth was Ruth, but they were the Pelfrey brothers.

Even now Ruth lives peaceful most of the time—she's a CNA at the hospital, shops in town, tends her own land. But every once in a while her boys show up, sometimes all at once.

Somebody goes to jail, usually Ellis, and the house will empty out for a time.

Every one of them's over thirty now. They stay for months in a row, drinking, sleeping late, never lifting a hand to help with anything. Once the first few weeks go by the routine picks up and business starts booming over there again. Ellis and Mitch have been arrested for methamphetamine half a dozen times each. Whenever they're staying with Ruth, vehicles come and go through the day, truck stereos blasting. Lot a times folks just drive up like they're at a fast food joint, in and out. But then one of the boys will get caught stealing a head gate or lawn chair or whatever else might be in reach. There'll be a fight. Somebody goes to jail, usually Ellis, and the house will empty out for a time.

No one knows why she tolerates them like that. A damn shame, but so it goes.

Instead of pulling into Ruth's driveway, I parked right in the middle of the street. Couldn't see Ellis anywhere, but Mitch and Danny had paired up against Henry Farler. Tarah and the girls were huddled on the porch in the background, looking scared as hell.

Danny's the youngest Pelfrey, few years behind Ellis. Always been a mouthy little cuss, but nowhere near as worrisome as the other two. Soon as I stepped up I told him to get his ass out of my sight, so he rushed off directly.

Getting the other two to settle down took a bit longer.

Henry Farler taught at the middle school back then, preached some at the Gambill Baptist Church on Saturday nights. He had a better head on his shoulders, so I told him go on back inside, I'd talk to him in a minute, but that got Mitch popping off again—"You letting him go" and "That ain't right goddamnit, after what he done" and "You need to be locking his ass up."

That last one stopped Henry in his tracks.

I said, "Nobody's being let go; just have to get you broke up so we can find out what's going on."

Mitch let his hands drop, took a step toward me. He had the same dry, sunken face as Ellis, same red sores from picking. His lips were peeled like he was thirsty all the time, but the lungs always sounded wet to me. "Ain't half right," he said. "How come ya'll get here so much quicker somebody calls on us?"

"Well, with you boys it's a cinch finding out who's doing what."

Henry clapped several times. "That's exactly right."

"I said go back inside, Henry."

The man did what I told him, but he clapped the whole way to his door. Mitch glared, hands shaking. I noticed the fingers had dry blood all over them.

I told him to come over to the car with me, but when we got there he splayed himself out on the hood like I was about to pat him down. That's how he acts with us most times, like he's still fifteen and impressing friends he don't even have any more. "Stand up, stop acting like a fool."

"Just beating you to it, ain't I?"

"Get off my car, right now," I said. "I can promise you something though—we catch you on their property like that again, you'll find your ass inside so quick you'll think it traveled through time. And no questions asked."

Mitch straightened and faced me. "What questions, man? None of you ever want to hear what we got to say."

"Was it you or Danny called in?"

"Why, didn't I do it right?" He fished in his pocket for a smoke.

"So you called then?"

"Momma asked me to. She been hunkered in the bedroom since it happened and we can't get her out."

I pointed behind him, toward Ruth's front porch. "She's right over there on the swing."

Mitch turned and saw Ruth sitting next to a defeated-looking Danny. "Oh. Well she's out now, but you should've seen her—so upset you wouldn't believe."

"I understand all that, it's a terrible thing. Upsets me and I wasn't even here." I offered him a light. He leaned in close, cupping his hands over the flame. "What I don't understand is why you boys charged over to Henry's like you did—"

"Because he done it—why the hell else?"

"Depends. You blaming him cause you hate him, or did any of you actually see him over at your momma's this time?"

Mitch stared at me a second, his mouth working the Newport around. "He done it. I feel it right in here."

"That don't answer my question."

"You give me a Bible and I'll swear to it right now," he said. "After all that other shit he done to us."

My head started throbbing a little then. "We're not going down that road today, so you best come to terms, you understand? I want to find—"

"See, but that shit right there just means you are letting him go again."

"Mitch, now I know you don't like it, but far as we're concerned Henry never did a thing wrong to anybody, except maybe disliking all the racket you guys make at night. And I can't blame him for that."

"Yeah, well...ya'll got your version. I know."

I could see him glazing over on that point already, so I decided to go another direction. "What'd you do with the head?"

He took a long drag, the smoke rolling up his face with the breeze. "Got it out back there."

That time of year the fallen leaves colored the place over, but she still had a few garden beds looking green.

Mitch just started walking, so I followed him. We hopped a little rainwater ditch and crossed over Ruth's front yard. That time of year the fallen leaves colored the place over, but she still had a few garden beds looking green. She was swinging on the porch, and I waved at her as we passed. She smiled, patting Danny on the leg.

Mitch took me round the side, right to the edge of that deep ravine that borders her property. Standing there, he said, "Pitched the damned thing over."

I about slapped him. "You threw it away?"

"No, you can still see it some. Right there, look."

The creek at the bottom must've been thirty feet below us. Little more than halfway down, the severed calf's head was caught in a nest of roots, wide eyed, mouth open some. Most the fur was brown, but it was flecked with enough white to make the bloodiness stand out, especially at the neck. It still looked fresh, but from that far down who the hell knows?

"Should we have held on to it?" Mitch asked.

"Would've helped some, don't you think?"

He glanced down the slope again. "Can't be more'n ten or fifteen feet."

"I'm not sliding my ass down after it, boy. Where's your head?"

"We wanted to get it away from Momma," he said. "I can tell you whatever cut it off's dull, though. Thing's got snags and tears all over it." Then he added, "The ears been sliced off too."

"Come again?"

Mitch nodded. "You heard right, sir. Ears are missing."

He pinched the tip of his cigarette and flicked the butt over the edge, like that was the last word on the subject.

I said, "No tags then."

"Nope."

About twenty feet to my right was Ruth's old woodshed. No windows, double doors cracked open a bit. I lowered my voice. "Ellis been around lately?"

Mitch said no, he hadn't seen him in months. "Since June maybe. Fact, last I heard he went down to Louisville cause...well, you know how it is round here, man—can't get a decent job to save your life no more. But I do remember he said something about finding one of those quick lube places hiring. He's always good with that stuff so I guess he must be doing okay."

"Hope so," I said. "He's not hiding over in that shed is he?"

Mitch cocked his head at me and frowned. "He ain't been here."

"Because he's in Louisville."

"Right."

I pretended to think it over. "Well, I know his license is suspended another two years."

"I don't know how in hell he got there, but he's there."

"Alright," I said. "So if I go open that door won't be nobody inside?"

"That's what I said, man."

"Just a lot of yard tools, stuff like that?"

This made him pause.

I turned and pointed at the shed. "Cause that's what you're saying, right? I look inside there I'm not gonna find anything I won't like..."

Mitch waited a second after I trailed off, then he started in about Ellis again.

I wasn't listening anymore.

The ravine wraps around the back of Ruth's house and I could see the gap between the trees where the ground dropped away. Beyond that was a clearing—one of the pastures of the Nance Farm. You couldn't reach the spot on foot without climbing a good bit, but looking out just then I suddenly knew I wouldn't need to search Ruth's shed for Ellis or anybody else.

Standing out in the clearing, seeming no taller than my thumb at that range, was the old boy himself: Amos Nance.

He was wearing jeans and a blue ball cap. Had on a hard-green camouflage coat that stood out against the fall colors all around him, and he must've realized it too cause he hustled away as soon as he caught me staring.

Felt my insides knot up a little then, knowing what I'd have to do next. I didn't wait for Mitch to finish talking, but it would've felt wrong to rush off right away, much as I wanted to. Proper thing was to ask Ruth how she was holding up, so I walked over to speak to her a minute, holding my keys so she'd know I had to hurry.

■ ■ ■

When the roads froze over the previous winter, I'd been part of a group ferrying groceries and medicine into the hollers for about a week. That was the last time I'd been to the Nances,' and I wasn't looking forward to this visit either.

Once I got a word in with Ruth, I turned back out onto Gambill Lane and took it east, trying to pick out the little gravel drive in all the brush. It was after eight and that narrow road was getting crowded. I saw Trudy Campbell, then Garret and Jean Wireman. Shep Reed zipped by way too fast in his USPS truck, but still managed to send a wave out the window at me. I remember a couple fellas came down from someplace outside Chicago a while back. One of them stopped by to see about some ordinance or other, talking about how friendly everybody was, and Joe said yeah, in Appalachia you save time just waving any time you walk anywhere.

Guess part of me wondered if I'd spot Amos Nance tearing down the road, waving casual like it was any other day. Big and old as he was, Amos could've gotten home by now if he hurried. Lot a land to cover though. They say in its prime that farm claimed more than a hundred acres, but that was before my time. Long as I've been around it's belonged to Amos and Willa alone. All told I think they had about twenty acres to themselves, what with the house, the small barn, couple decrepit outbuildings.

Enough pastureland for the thirty or so cows they owned too.

I found the turnoff and paused there long enough to update Joe over the radio.

The Nance house looked empty when I pulled up—blinds drawn, cars missing.

I parked a ways back so I'd have to walk the last ten yards or so, give them a few extra minutes to spy me coming. The front yard was grooved up with muddy tire tracks. On the porch, a pair of muck boots still slick with dew.

I knocked politely.

Willa peeked her silver head around the curtain twice before opening the front door, unsmiling.

I said, "Morning, Willa."

She shook her head. "I know. Come on in."

Like someone exasperated and resigned, she shoved the door wide and skulked in ahead of me.

"Want me to lock this?"

Willa said, "Don't matter," so I turned the latch and followed her toward the dining room. It was dim and smelled like a week's worth of exhaling. I didn't pretend to look around and Willa didn't seem to expect me to.

"Want a coffee?"

I'd always known Amos Nance to be a decisive, deliberate sort of a man, but as a crook he wasn't too elusive.

I said yes. "Lots of sugar if it's no problem."

She went right to it. I walked over to a yellow card table and pulled out a pair of folding chairs, made them face each other. Then I sat in the sturdier of the two, unbuttoned my jacket so the uniform showed.

Someone was scurrying around in a nearby part of the house. Any other day the clumsiness of it all might've got me laughing. I'd always known Amos Nance to be a decisive, deliberate sort a man, but as a crook he wasn't too elusive.

Willa came back in. "Had to start a new pot."

"Oh, don't go to no trouble," I said, then when she tried to sit in the other chair, "No, no. That's not for you."

"Huh?"

"Where's he at, Willa?"

She rolled her eyes. "Who'd that be?"

I stared at her till she got uncomfortable. She said, "Went out walking."

"Oh, I—I'm sure of that," I said. "Saw him back in the east pasture just before I came here."

The old woman crossed her arms, shrugged.

"That's only about twenty minutes ago, Willa."

"If you say so."

"Hm. Went out barefoot did he?"

"What?"

"Right." I raised my voice. "Amos? Would you come in here please?"

Willa sighed. I saw right off she was probably pissed at Amos more than I was, but I tut-tutted her. "False witness, Mrs. Nance."

She snapped her eyes up at me. "Wasn't no lie—he did go walking."

I cleared my throat. "Right now, Amos."

A minute later the old boy came out looking the way an off-season Santa might—silver hair, beard thick as lather. I guess the grey sweats and green flannel shirt were supposed to throw me off, but I could tell he'd just got them on.

We greeted each other civil and I motioned to the empty chair.

Amos glared at Willa when he waddled past her.

"Don't give me the eye. I told you I wasn't gonna lie at all." She turned back to the kitchen.

He waved her off and sat down, a bunch of his old hinges popping as he did.

It was even harder to face the man as an authority figure this time round. We didn't say anything at first and I knew I'd have to initiate.

Every now and then I'd see Willa in town, often enough to stay familiar, but with Amos it was different. You didn't hear much from him those days. Years back he got around, even hosted a welding rodeo at the spring fairs, but when Perry Gravel laid him off he sort of receded into the landscape.

Willa clattered some dishes around in the sink. I took it as a cue to start. "How the hands doing?"

Amos laced his fingers across his belly. He'd gotten so wide his arms had to be almost straight for his hands to reach.

I smiled, tried something different. "Read my mind, sir."

"How's that?"

"Tell me what I'm thinking."

"Well I...I got no idea."

"We really gonna go that route?"

He shrugged the same way Willa had, so I decided to tenderize him. "Okay," I said. "Thing is somebody went and made my morning real awkward today. Stuck a calf's head on Ruth Pelfrey's doorstep, about upset that woman to death, stoked up a feud across the street probably outlast everyone in the county. So what I'm thinking is that same somebody's got to start talking to me right now or he'll be looking at a mess of charges. Trespassing, vandalism, harassment, animal cruelty—"

Willa came back, handed me a mug with a chip in the handle. I thanked her, took a sip. This time she stood in the doorway behind Amos, waiting.

I put the mug on the table. "I'll say it one more time, sir. Read my mind."

He started getting fidgety, thumbs not so much twiddling as sparing with each other. After staring off a bit, he said. "Calves was already dead."

I nodded. "That's a start. How'd that ha—"

"They done poisoned our creek."

"Is that right?"

He nodded.

Behind him, Willa shook her head.

“Calf was in the water?” I asked.

“No, up a ways on the ridge. Been acting off the last week or so and they all drink out that creek.”

“Other cows sick too?”

He shook his head. “Not so far, no.”

“You have any stillborn with that last lot?”

“Not a one.”

“That’s—if you think that, take a water sample up to the school and see what Grady says about it.”

“Don’t need all that,” he said, all indignant like. “I know it.”

“That’s a theme today,” I told him. “Gut feelings never stand up at the courthouse, Amos.”

“We found thirty-seven bottles up the creek not ten yards from our fence—drain cleaner, antifreeze, thinners. Lord knows how long it’s been leeching out, and I don’t need no gut feeling to tell me what those boys’re cooking out there in that shed all the damned time neither. Everybody knows it, you know it, but they’re still doing it.”

“Ellis ain’t been over there since June.”

“Mitch feed you that?”

“No, Ruth said so herself. Not since he and those other two lit that camper in Buford.”

Amos considered this, his face relaxing some. “It does pain me to think I upset her. She’s a lovely woman.”

“I know she is, but everybody over there thinks it’s the Farlers who put that head at her doorstep.”

Amos shook his head. “They got nothing to do with it.”

He said it like he was easing my pain or something. “So what? You stirred up a hell of a mess. Ruth seems okay now, but they say it frightened half that woman’s memories away.”

Amos paused. “Didn’t mean it for her.”

“It’s her house, what the hell’d you think was gonna happen? She wakes up and it’s the first damned thing she sees in the morning.”

"Suppose if I...had it to do over again—"

"They don't need any more reasons to go at each other over there."

"Already said it ain't got nothing to do with them across the way, didn't I? But if nobody else is gonna step up to her boys—"

"Amos, those dummies don't know it's you—they probably don't even remember you live back here," I said. "And think if they did. Is that something you want?"

"How do you mean?"

"Suppose I was to tell Mitch you did it? What'd that—now I ain't threatening you none, so you best drop that nasty look. I mean as part of my duty, say I was to set the record straight over there, cause you know what—I might do it. Understand? If for no other reason than to make things more peaceful for those two little girls, cause I see shit like what's happened today and they're my first concern. See where I'm coming from?"

Amos said he did.

"Imagine all the trouble Ellis and them could cause if I ever have to give them a reason to remember you. Think that'd go over well?"

"No. Reckon it wouldn't."

Willa was still standing in the kitchen doorway looking at me. I said, "You already say all this?"

"Mostly," she said. "Last night when he was cutting them up, but he don't listen to me none."

Amos mumbled, "Say something worth listening to."

Willa stretched an arm out and swatted him lightly on the side of the head.

I told her not to. Then to Amos, "Where're the cars at?"

Willa said, "Out beside the barn. Fool tore up the yard trying to hide 'em from you few minutes before you showed up."

The three of us sat quiet after that. Couple years back Amos got tired of the Pelfreys ripping up and down the road all hours, so the silly bastard tried to light Ellis's pickup on fire. Truck bed was full of cleaning supplies and all he managed to do was burn his hands up. He got back to his house before we arrived with the fire unit. Wasn't much to do—just a big puddle of melted plastic in the truck. Pretty sure Ellis still drives it, with or without his suspension. I found Amos when I was asking around the neighborhood later that morning, sitting fully clothed in the bathtub, hands all blistered.

Kept his involvement to myself that time cause I figured he'd punished himself enough, but this. Well, I didn't know what to do.

"I ain't gonna give you the three strikes speech. And I'm sorry about the calf, but you cannot pull this kind crap, and you know it. If you think the water's gone sour, have it tested. Grady and them find it's like you say, then we can do something."

Amos stood up, maybe sensing I was winding down. "Okay."

Willa wasn't leaning against the doorway no more. She was upright, looking between the two of us with some intent I didn't catch at first, so I said, "Don't beat him too bad now."

Amos smiled. "Oh, we been married for centuries, we'll be fine—"

"Amos," Willa said, "don't you dare."

Her tone was the kind that made me stand up, especially since Amos flinched.

"Am I gonna have to tell him?" she said

I asked, "What's that?"

She came up and nudged him, but he just looked at the floor.

I told him to sit back down and he did, all slumped over and disappointed. "Tell me what?"

Amos said, "Already told you."

"Okay, so tell me again."

He scratched at his beard. "It was two calves died."

"What the hell's that supposed to mean?"

Amos breathed deep, but didn't answer.

Willa spoke up. "He drove over to Shep Reed's about six this morning and asked him to take it to the Pelfreys with the mail."

I said, "Take what with the mail?"

I was staring right at him, but he wouldn't meet my eyes.

"Stuck it in a box lined with garbage bags," Willa said.

Even closer to his face, I said, "Shep's taking what with the mail?"

All Amos said was, "Poisoned my damned creek."

■ ■ ■

I stopped the cruiser beside that NO OUTLET sign on Locust again.

This time the Pelfreys and Henry Farler were in the street, shouting and flailing their arms in the air. Ruth and Tarah watched from the sidelines, probably trying to settle things down, but it looked like they couldn't get a word in edgewise. At one point Mitch and Henry started kicking something back and forth across the blacktop at each other. I knew it was the second calf's head.

I picked up the handset. "I'm pulling up now."

On the other end, Joe said, "Sure you don't want me to head over to the Nances' place?"

"No. Amos insisted on driving himself in."

A pause. "Think we can rely on that?"

"Yeah. Just make sure someone's there to meet him. If it takes him more than an hour or so we'll see."

"It's after nine, we're all in now," Joe said. "Need one of us to come out to you?"

"Maybe," I said. "Actually, let me try and handle it first, then I'll get back with you."

"Well, as long as you're sure. What're they doing this time?"

I watched Henry lift and hurl the head onto Ruth's front yard. Within seconds Mitch was running to fetch it.

I shook my head. "Just being neighborly." ■

STARTING OUT TOGETHER IN WEST VIRGINIA

driving to meet you in that mountain town
road canopied with trees
sun through, flashes
of river running alongside

the way you looked the same
felt the same, but
an odor on your breath, clothes reeking
shell forming around
my quivering inside

interplay of green and light
blue silk, the nightgown in my bag
bought specially for this

later, laughter and loud music
dances with men
flashes of jealousy, flashes
of guns, your anger
carrying me to the rented room

heart racing at remembering
the planning, hands held across
smooth diner table
the thrill of seeing your car
after all this time

slap of water under this crude lodge
clack of metal, hammer hidden
under your thumb
blue silk flying, steel
cold and smooth at my temple
please...please finish
finally, maybe you'll sleep

gurgle of water, nip of night
rush of wind blowing my hair

gun set aside, you breathe
heavy at last
I breathe, I can leave now
still I lie
next to you as day breaks

JULIA CAMPBELL JOHNSON

RUNNING AWAY

Without a mother's advice, I gather
what I'll need. At a store in town
I look for something with appeal
for an experienced man. A nightgown–
silk is supposed to be sexy.
The clerk is Rob Foster's mother.
Her teenaged son I have dated now and then.
She tells me as she rings the sale about
his college girlfriend, about their visit
planned for spring. I say nothing,
knowing I'll be gone.

JULIA CAMPBELL JOHNSON

FULL MOON, BLACK NIGHT

Solemn moon between two hills,
mounds of deep blue turned black by night.
Along the ridge a cavalry in silhouette–
spruce, pine. Moon fixed in relief
on a sky greyed with stripes.
Lone star, grip of heaven.

JULIA CAMPBELL JOHNSON

AN *APPALACHIAN HERITAGE* INTERVIEW WITH

CONNIE MAY FOWLER

A Million Fragile Bones, bestselling novelist Connie May Fowler's new memoir, is the story of a life connected irrevocably to the natural world: in this case, the Gulf Coast of Florida and the wild sandbar where Fowler once lived. Published in April, it is also a story told within the framework of the 2010 Deepwater Horizon explosion and its devastating aftermath. As in her earlier memoir, *When Katie Wakes* (2002), Fowler explores the trauma of abuse, the power of memory, and the fragile, indelible ties between human beings and the earth.

Appalachian Heritage interviewed Connie May Fowler through an email exchange. Western North Carolina-based novelist and newspaper columnist Katherine Scott Crawford conducted the interview with Fowler, who writes from her home on an island off the Yucatecan coast of Mexico.

■■■

KATHERINE SCOTT CRAWFORD: This is your second memoir; *When Katie Wakes* was published in 2002. Would you talk about the life you've led since the publication of that first memoir, and the decision to write *A Million Fragile Bones* within the framework of the Deepwater Horizon explosion and its aftermath?

CONNIE MAY FOWLER: Well, *a lot* has happened since 2002. In the intervening time, I published four more books. My first marriage ended. For a long time, I lived alone at Alligator Point—just me and my dogs and all that wildlife. I continued my involvement in domestic violence awareness, child abuse prevention, and environmental activism. Eventually, I remarried a wonderful guy, Bill Hinson. Through each passage, I continued my teaching journey. All-in-all, I lived a meager life in terms of wealth but a rich one if our gauge is happiness. Then on April 20, 2010, BP's Macondo Deep Water oil rig blew up in the Gulf of Mexico, changing the Gulf and my life forever.

In the months before the disaster, I had been tinkering with a memoir about place, about the semi-wilderness I lived in and how the isolation shaped me. My publicist at the time, Tanisha Sabine Christie, had been needling me to write it all down. One day, in response, I sent her an email that began, "I live on the edge of the world." She immediately emailed back, saying, *That's it! That's the beginning of your new book!*

I was probably twenty pages in, trying to figure out the shape and intent of the book, when the rig blew. As I said, the disaster changed my entire world. Suddenly, the place I loved with the ferocity of blood, the place that had taught me and healed me, was under twenty-four-hour assault by one of the most dangerous, but crucial, substances we possess: oil.

Just like that, because of the greed and ineptitude of one multinational, mega-billion-dollar company, I had a different book. And, sadly, a different life. Events forced the memoir to address not only what had brought me to the sandbar and the many lessons learned in nature's isolation, but the exactitudes and ramifications of what happens when everything is blown asunder.

KSC: Your works are marked by a distinct concern with place, a practice that is an intrinsic aspect of being a Southern storyteller with Appalachian roots. In the book, you write, "My friends share a healthy sense of place. Perhaps this is why we love each other. None of them bat an eye when I gaze out at the sea and say, 'This is my church.'" What role does place play in *A Million Fragile Bones*, beyond the traditional sense of place as setting?

CMF: Place is everything in *A Million Fragile Bones*. You see me returning to St. Augustine time and again as I haplessly try to recapture the town as it was when my father was alive,

Connie May Fowler

and most specifically, regain a sense of the area's natural abundance. When that turns out to be folly, I migrate to the semi-wilderness of the northern Gulf Coast and Alligator Point, a place I believe my father would have loved and would have felt at home in. I immerse myself in the rhythms of place in order to heal and create a bond with a father I barely knew. Place—nature unfettered—becomes my godhead. When it is destroyed by the worst manmade disaster in United States' history, I, too, in ways great and small, am destroyed.

I am a person whose personal history wavers as if it perpetually dances behind old, leaded glass. I knew only one grandparent and she died when I was five. My father died when I was six and my mother, who descended into madness in the aftermath of my father's death but who did, by God, the best job she could have given the circumstances, died when I was eighteen. Early on, I sensed place was the only thing I had—the only constant—and if St. Augustine was developing too quickly for me to hang onto that sense of place, I would find some nook or cranny where it still existed. I considered Appalachia—my mother's home; she was from Grundy—but I knew none of her people. And, to be honest, it was my father's sense of place I craved. It was a sense of place that for a brief few years we shared. I was lucky to find Alligator Point and its wilderness coast and equally lucky to have lived there for twenty years. As I answer you, it suddenly makes sense to me why I weep whenever I talk about the loss.

KSC: Christ images abound in your descriptions of your father—crowns, crooked, thorny and otherwise, appear. Your mother tells you that your father is a drunk. You write that your memories are "wholly different than my half-brother's," and that your older sister "retains no

memories." What role do you think memory plays in your memoir in particular? Do you think we can trust our own memories, and does it really matter if we do?

CMF: It is no accident that the word "memoir" contains within it the seed of memory. What are we if not a collection of memory and experience? Our conundrum is that we all perceive the same event differently, which is pretty wild. You know about the Innocence Project, yes? Using DNA to determine innocence or guilt, their researchers were able to overturn seventy-three percent of 239 convictions that had relied on eye-witness testimony. We never, to borrow an old phrase, truly see eye-to-eye. It's as if we're all operating inside our own private holograms. But that is all we have. Experience. Memory. Our individual perceived truths that, in the best of times, coalesce with that of others. As writers, we have no choice: We relate our memories, in both fiction and nonfiction, as honestly as we can, shaky voices and all.

Without humans telling our truths, we become less humane, less reflective, less empathetic. Telling our stories is a necessary component of being human. Think how thin, how anemic, a child's life would be if her parents did not fill her up with story. It's a wondrous moment of symbiosis: As the child receives the tale, memories begin to form.

KSC: You say that "the shack is my heart." What does a person do when their heart is so irrevocably damaged?

CMF: In time, you get back on your feet by any means possible. You put one foot in front of the other. And you find a new heart or find a way to live with the damaged one. It might take years, but the journey is the heart. Figuring that out is sometimes only possible in the quiet, wise lens of the long view.

KSC: *A Million Fragile Bones* is billed as "a love song to the natural world and a cry of anger and grief at its ruin for the sake of corporate profits." But I think it is also a meditation on what it means to be fully human in connection with the natural world: to share its DNA, to be a participant on a cellular level. Can you talk about that?

CMF: I love that you use the phrase "to share its DNA" because that is precisely the situation. At the risk of going Carl Sagan on us, we truly are made of stardust. All of this—the human, the fish, the bird, the wolf, the tree, the stone, the orchid—we are related. We are all part of the same mysterious, sacred tapestry of life. I think much of the existential angst experienced by so many people today is because they no longer recognize this. In the book, I muse, "When humans decided we were not of the animal kingdom—when we decided to translate a biblical Aramaic word as 'dominion over' rather than 'caretaker of'—did we seal our fate as well as that of our planet?"

The difference between dominator and caretaker is vast. If we are caretakers, we are braided into the lives we care for. We, in some ways, become one. The viability and vitality of life becomes our first priority. Oil companies? Coal companies? They dominate. Life is a secondary concern to profits. I am not overstating our current peril. If we don't change our thinking and realize our fate is tied to the butterfly's, then our one and only home will become inhospitable to life as we know it. We will all be that polar bear trying to balance on a melting slab of ice, a slab that once was an iceberg.

KSC: The memoir is set mostly in Alligator Point, Florida, and you do a masterful job of creating a world both painful in its beauty but also rich and enveloping. Mother Nature looms large. As a reader, I found it bittersweet—and just plain hard at times—to continue reading about and falling in love with this place, knowing what was going to happen. How did you manage the intensity of that back-and-forth between love and grief, or love and anger, when you were writing?

CMF: The memoir is inherently complex because I had to address why I fell in love with Alligator Point and that northern coastal region of Florida. It wasn't just, *Wow! This is pretty*. It was deep, deep stuff about longing and loss, finding home and finding peace. It was, in many ways, about the nature of grace. And once that was on the page, I had to dive into the newly dawned darkness of the spill, a horror which grew exponentially daily. The process was made more difficult by the fact that much of the memoir was written while it was happening and in the immediate aftermath, so I really had to be on my toes in terms of truth and craft.

I've never taken to the pen with a faint heart. Writing is an act of courage by people who know if they don't tell their truths, their hearts will explode. If the process turns you into a visage of Edvard Munch's *The Scream*—and it almost always does—so be it. As a writer, you always know the momentary pain of creation beats the alternative. When it comes to creating art, I will choose pain over the void of non-creation every time. And the payoff is that by the end of the process, you are no longer *The Scream*. You are a hero, a shaman, because you have created beauty in truth.

KSC: Readers know from earlier in the memoir that you've had experience with abuse. Later, you write that BP's

Fowler's memoir was published in April.

behavior during the oil spill disaster is "beginning to feel abusive." Can you explain what you mean by that?

CMF: Abusers have a lot of things in common. They gas-light their victims. They behave as if they are the wronged party and you are silly or stupid or insane for pointing out their aggressions. They lie without any apparent conscience. They are bullies. And they destroy beauty. BP executives, with help from the United States government, did all of that. They told us there was no oil on our beaches, yet we were walking through it. While animals died in our arms, they ran millions of dollars in advertising, claiming the Gulf was A-Okay. They lied about how much oil was gushing into the sea. They tried to turn sons against fathers and neighbors against neighbors, encouraging us to rat out our loved ones if we suspected they were filing false claims. Hired trolls ghosted social media, calling us liars and worse.

As evidence mounted all around as to the absolute hell the oil and dispersant were wreaking, we were told we had no idea what we were talking about, that our new reality was a figment of our imaginations. By mid-summer of 2010, the federal government said private citizens could be slapped with a Class-D felony and a $40,000 fine if they ventured within sixty-five feet of boom, oiled animals, oiled shorelines, and anything else related to the disaster, which by happenstance of where I lived put me in violation twenty-four-seven. While the health of Gulf Coast residents—especially that of the fishermen who went into the oiled sea to try to contain the mess so that they could work again—Tony Hayward, the CEO of BP at the time of the spill—griped that he just wanted his life back. Yet the lives of those of us affected—wildlife and human—were expendable. It was as if the oil giant considered us little more than collateral damage. And let us not forget, eleven men died on that rig as a result of BP's negligence and not one individual has been or will be held accountable in our courts.

KSC: You now live in Mexico, in the Yucatan. What led you there?

CMF: We moved to the Yucatan from Florida and are now living on an island just off the Yucatecan coast. Although, it needs to be said that I maintain my Florida residency and U.S. citizenship. My husband and I have simply flung our nets a little further afield.

My fascination with the Yucatan began long ago, while listening to meteorologists continually refer to the peninsula during hurricane season. And then, sitting on that beach at Alligator Point and watching the bird migrations and monarch butterfly migrations, I did my homework and traced their journeys to the Yucatan. I stared for hours across that expanse of water, wondering what was on the far shore. This leads us back to one of your first questions, the one about place. And also, the one about the broken heart. We came here to immerse ourselves once more in a sacred sense of place, of nature abundant, and thereby heal our broken hearts.

KSC: In Part One of the book, you recount the day a PBS crew filmed at your shack on Alligator Point. You write, "You either tell everything or you tell a lie." After everything that has happened, from that day to this one, do you still feel the same?

CMF: Absolutely. I don't know if it's the writer part of me or the battered little girl part of me, maybe both, but I have a need to try to tell the whole truth lest the Earth tilt off its axis. And that depth of truth-telling is impossible most of the time. That is why when I am with a group of strangers, I nearly always go mute. Telling the whole story is impossible in the width of a handshake. Although, that might be a pretty great short story...

KSC: Do you ever think you'll return to Alligator Point?

CMF: I don't know. I don't think I'm ready yet. The two people I bought the house from and who became surrogate parents to me, owned the other house on the property that the sale divvied up. They came down from time to time from Tallahassee and their visits were always illuminating in terms of the shack's history and that of the Point. I planned to visit them as soon as the book was done. That was the goal: Get the book done, thereby achieving a measure of peace, and then go see them. That felt right. I knew they would buffer me from the inevitable pain of return and the entire affair would become a celebration of sorts. But they passed on before any of that could happen. I am coming to terms with the fact that with their passing, my familial connection to Alligator Point is gone.

Recently, the shack fell into new ownership and the person, very kindly, extended an invitation for me to visit whenever I wanted. She sent photos of some of the work they've done. It looks wonderful, as if it again is in the hands of people who love it.

But I have a voice in my head. It keeps whispering, "Move on." ■

DAY LILY

Each year, the centurial black walnut
threatens to expire,

yet flowers branch by branch, bud by bud,
magisterial in its hour.

Sunlit moss berms Linville Creek.
Yellow rock tablets lull the stream.

Upon the aged plank bridge,
in velvet sprawls a mink.

You, Lily, feathery, fluted,
pistil and stamen, bathe

there at the bank, like Artemis,
For just a day, gazing

at the clouds hovering the ridge
beyond which dreams the next life

vaulted in the firmament.
You burst into this world through desire,

that alone your imprimatur.
Yet make no mistake:

you are permitted entry through grace.
You may not begn for this pittance,

however ephemeral, burning as you are.
It befalls you. I should stop now.

A Day Lily does not want for a man,
but sainthood, ablaze

for a lone revolution on earth's axis,
then offering itself in sacrifice,

kin to those brazen red-headed martyrs—
trussed pendent to your stem,

puckered, collapsed parasol,
loved but once in flaming thrall.

JOSEPH BATHANTI

TRAPDOOR SPRING

All was spiny loneliness of branch and bark,
then, in an instant, all was a threat of bursting
liveliness, nothing but the night's dark blur

of promise hinting as to what waited for us
in the day's light, summoned out of sleep by

a long rain, the sun's alchemy working a soil
and root palette of possibility up through
thawing ice branch, suddenly splashing surprise

along the mountainsides, the rumor of spring
conspiring to usher in our wakeful laughter.

LARRY THACKER

THE LETTERS

JANET S. HOLLOWAY

Let's go in here and talk," she said, guiding my shoulder toward her bedroom. Granny Bill closed the door and sat on the small stool that fronted her oversized maple dresser. She fidgeted with her hand mirror and comb while I looked around, not knowing whether to sit or stand. I settled on the sunny spot on the floor, across from her bed. The three-paneled mirror on the dresser reflected her softness from every side.

"They's some things we have to talk about that ain't easy to talk about. Do you understand?" She bent down to look me in the eye.

I shrugged, "I guess so."

I could tell this was going to be a very grown-up conversation, something of a challenge for this eleven-year-old.

"Now, your daddy's a good man, Janet. Sometimes he don't act like it, but he means well, you understand?"

I nodded, agreeing with her, even though from an early age, I was aware of a strangeness in my parents. They weren't like my friends' parents, with my mother disappearing every so often and my dad somehow persuading or coercing her back to the family. We'd adjust, she'd rearrange the all the furniture I'd placed, and then be off again.

This time, as soon as my dad left West Virginia for Tampa to work for a friend of his, mom left in a flash with her cousin Pauline, headed for West Palm Beach and what they considered the good life—working as waitresses in a steakhouse. Nobody needing her or telling her what to do. She left my younger brother Danny and me behind with Granny, with strict instructions not to say a word to Dad about her whereabouts. She had a lot of rules: "Because I said so," was a favorite. Then there was: "When I tell you to keep your mouth shut, you keep your mouth shut." I was trying to remember how long she'd been gone when Granny pulled at my shirt.

"Are you listening to me, girl? He's a good man, but his coming in and taking you and Danny out of school today... well...that wasn't right," she hesitated.

In the silence, I waited, studying a filmy rainbow on the wall and following it to its source, the late afternoon light bouncing off the metal strip of her pine handkerchief box and spreading across the big pink roses on the wall. Today, the room smelled of Pond's cold cream and my own sweat.

Earlier today, my classroom had the smell of sweet lilac. I sat there, with the other sixth graders, trying to pay attention to the geography lesson about North and South America, but I was daydreaming and inhaling the lilacs blooming outside the half-open window. "There ain't nothing sweeter than lilacs and peonies," Granny would say, "except you!"

North and South America got dropped like a bag of dirt when my father walked into the classroom. His sudden appearance startled me, as he stood at the edge of a row of wooden desks, looking down each one until he found me.

"Janet, get your books and come with me."

Mrs. Mercer tried to say something, but he cut her off, "She won't be back."

His sudden appearance startled me, as he stood at the edge of a row of wooden desks, looking down each one until he found me.

My surprise was stung with fear and excitement at seeing him after so many months.

"Somebody must be bad sick, for him to be here," I thought to myself and hurriedly pulled the books and papers out of my desk, carefully folding my book report down the middle the way Mrs. Mercer liked. I was already disappointed that I might not hear her tell the class how much she enjoyed my carefully worded report.

She looked at me questioningly as I handed it to her. My best friend Phyllis mouthed "I'll see you later," and I nodded, not knowing what to expect.

My brother Danny was waiting in the hallway, trying to balance his books, his Superman lunch box and his baseball bat in his thin ten-year-old arms. He gave me a confused look and I just shrugged.

My mouth tasted like I'd sucked on a piece of metal, and swallowing wasn't helping. My father was quiet on the drive to the farm, saying, "We'll talk about it at home."

In the back seat, I hugged my books to my chest, hoping they would keep me from floating away. Danny sat close, rocking from side to side. My dad dropped us off by the farm gate, saying, "Go start packing. I'll be right back; I'm going for cigarettes."

Granny cleared her throat, raked her fingers over her knees and took a deep breath, "What I'm trying to say is, you know how your momma and daddy argue all the time, and your daddy had to go work in Florida when the mines closed down last year?"

The words rushed out before she could call them back. She pulled at the bodice of her house dress and blew air over her breasts. Nobody ever talked about those arguments between my parents, but here she was saying the words. I had a spasm of courage and turned to her.

"Well, yes, but nobody ever explained why mom and Aunt Pauline went to Florida in the first place—the whole other side of the state from where he was. Nobody ever explained that to me."

I locked my fingers into a steeple and flushed, fearing my words had sounded harsh.

"Honey, that's what I'm trying to tell you."

"What?"

"Your daddy found out that your mother and Pauline were down there. I don't know who told him. Anyway he's mad at me for sending your mother's letters to him, the way I did, you know, in that other envelope."

She pulled a handkerchief from her bosom, wiped at a dusting of face powder on the dresser, and then used it to pat her neck dry. She avoided looking at me.

"And?"

The facts were making me dizzy and impatient.

"And, so, he's taking you and Danny away, down to where your mother is. He says you all are leaving tomorrow morning."

She covered her eyes with her hand, as if these words were too much for her. "I'm sorry, honey; I'm so sorry. You know how your mother can be when she sets her mind to something. I didn't know what else to do."

I knew this letter business had been going on, but nobody ever explained anything. Granny would get a letter from my mother, and there'd be a special envelope in it, stamped and addressed to my dad. Granny would put it out for the mailman. When I'd ask why mom wasn't sending the letter herself, Granny would just say, "It's for me to know and you to find out, little girl!"

Sometimes in mom's letter there were two crisp one dollar bills for Danny and me. Granny's *tsk-tsking* at this always made me think she disapproved of children having that much money. It was only later I understood her displeasure with my mother on all fronts. I sat there now, knees up against my chest, more confused than ever, inhaling my own smell and trying to cross my toes over one another. I didn't know what to say. I just rocked back and forth and crossed my toes.

Granny stood up, "You're going to have to go with him, honey. He's your daddy. And..." she pulled her soft pink dress away from where it had lodged in the crevices of her body, "we have so much to do to get ready! Let's get going, girl!"

As the tears welled up, I opened my eyes wide, trying to stretch my face so they wouldn't fall. It wasn't that I couldn't cry in front of her; I just didn't want to cry over this.

"I'm not going," I coughed. "I'm staying here."

She pulled me to her, "Oh, honey, I'm so sorry. I wish that daughter of mine would grow up. She's hurt you children terribly."

The tears raced down my sunburned face, crusting salt lines in their path. "I'm not going," I said. "I'm staying with you."

"Child, I wish you could. But he's your daddy and he's made up his mind and...uh oh, here he comes, driving up the hill." She shook me softly and wiped my face with her handkerchief. "Go wash up. Don't let him see you this way."

I ran out the back door of the house, past Danny who was eating crackers and grape jelly on the side porch, further up the hill to a limestone boulder just this side of the top of the

I was always happy lying on this rock at night, after dinner and chores were done, studying the stars and wondering about boys and heaven and poems...

hill. I was always happy lying on this rock at night, after dinner and chores were done, studying the stars and wondering about boys and heaven and poems I'd read—all sorts of things—without anxiety, without fear.

In the dimming light, I saw my dad walk up on the porch, flick his cigarette away from the house and go inside. I couldn't tell if he said anything to my brother or not. I stood there against the rock, in the shadow of old cedars, on the edge of a drama about to unfold.

There were no words to explain all the feelings I had at that moment—the hurt and confusion and fear, all bound up with dread—that unspoken caution about what was to come, waiting for the next shoe to drop, as it inevitably would.

How could Granny not stand up for me? Couldn't she see what lay ahead for Danny and me? I needed her and she was stepping back. And here was my father, whom I hadn't seen in months. He was like a stranger, demanding I leave the only place where I felt safe and protected. He wanted to take us from granny's where I slept peacefully and woke up to hear her talking about the farm chores of the day and where I knew what was expected of me. Here he was, wanting to take us out of school and away from safety, drive a thousand miles to confront my mother with her tricks and lies. God knows she was full of them, more than he even suspected.

I thought back to the times when I was about seven and she'd wake me in the middle of the night, asking if I'd like an ice cream. No matter what I said, we'd end up at some beer joint down the road. Me, half asleep in my pajamas in a corner booth; her, drinking beer and dancing with some man.

"Now, if your daddy wakes up when we get home, you tell him you wanted an ice cream," she would say.

Why couldn't I fight my mother then? Why didn't I refuse to go along, refuse to be part of her schemes? Because I was seven? Because another one of those rules said "obey your parents, no matter what"? Or because I was, at that time, inescapably bound to her: recognizing that she always won out over my father and my grandmother. Safety lay in going along, not making waves. None of the grown-ups could deny her; how could I? Her conspiracies trumped the truth every time.

Why didn't he just go face her himself, once he found out where she was? Why did he have to drag us along and throw us in her face? I wondered if they knew or even cared how their craziness affected me and Danny, and, just as quickly, answered my own question: "children are to be seen and not heard." We were irrelevant at best.

I began to wonder if I had the same genes that drove my mother's need for excitement and control, for that adrenaline rush that came with each win, that feeling of being alive. Did I secretly, unconsciously enjoy the excitement, the danger?

I couldn't manage all these thoughts at once, but neither could I hide from the basic and immediate truth. Having my brother and me in tow gave my father the upper hand. One more time, he'd get her back, no matter the cost.

"Oh, god, leave me out of it!" I said out loud, wondering how could I escape them? Where could I go, if Granny insisted I leave with him? My chest hurt with the knowledge that she wouldn't stand up for me. I didn't like it and yet I understood it: because they were my parents, not her. That had to be the reason; why else would she let me go? That, and the fact that her interference with my mother's will had seldom held fast over the years.

"Your mother's pitiful, Janet," she'd say. "She's sick or she wouldn't be acting this way." As if being sick made it all okay.

The quiet of that darkening, moonless night, the mist settling over the fields and orchard, brought me to my senses. Reluctantly, exhaling a deep breath, I admitted I had no choice but to go. My back ached from leaning into the cold rock, and I stood to stretch.

"Janet, come help me with dinner." I could see my grandmother calling from the porch. "It's getting dark and your daddy's hungry."

I walked down to the house. Dad sat at the table with Danny, telling him what to write on the tablet in front of him. He motioned for me to sit and slid a sheet of lined paper to me.

"I want you to write your mother a letter. Tell her how awful she is for deserting you and Danny. We'll give her the letters when we get there."

Deserted? I didn't feel I'd been deserted. I protested, "Why are you making us do this? I don't want to write a letter!"

"Sit down and write the letter," he insisted.

No place to run, no place to hide, I slammed my fist on the table and screamed one last time, "I don't want to go!"

"You're going," he said, his face fiercer than I could remember, "so sit down and write the damned letter."

Granny busied herself at the stove, shaking her head, not looking our way.

I reached for the pencil. ■

SNAKE CANE

Norman Amos

Sometimes Virginia Creeper,
a tendril of honeysuckle or wild
grape, will wind around the limb
of a young hickory and, as both grow,
squeeze its spiral into the wick.
Old women who tap the ground
before they walk, ready to rap danger
on its head, tobacco farmers well-versed
in the habits of serpents, carry such twisted sticks.
Search for them in our tick-breeding woods—
mumbo-jumbo of undergrowth, full-throated
green, saplings bent, knitted together with briars,
mayapples pushing past skunk cabbages
and then the dying that comes with the first frost,
oak leaves baked brown and sycamore platters
curling inward on the ground, poison ivy
dried up to one hairy vine thick as a man's wrist.
Step down into the furrows of an old road bed,
deer stand draped in black quiet as wildness itself,
easy to miss among the doe-legged trees.
Daddy sang, *I'm the man who rode the mule
around the world,* voice ragged as a forgotten
trotline. *I was born ten thousand years ago.*
Bright leaf tobacco cured in the smoke.
I tended the low fires. Black night rustled
up close to me and sometimes I caught a glimpse
of a thing. The cedars breathed by the fence row.
You have to find the wood first, branch of desire

wound round with grapevine, nearly strangled
and then: growing on anyway.
I'll paint it like a shining rattlesnake,
body spinning up the stick.
Your hand will rest on its head,
devil eyes subdued, looking up at you,
fangs following the way the handle bends,
benign in their whiteness, polished by hand-
sweat and the oily traces of a hundred dusty hunts—
mountain feists yapping along with the rhythm
of the staff, rabbit cry dark as dried blood
in the autumn wind. Silent rattles cover the end
that hits the dirt, seeking strikes
in high summer's high grass,
feeling a human way through deep leaves,
hollow-wise, rocks holding heat,
or shaking the snake-rich shadows of blackberry canes
before the hand reaches in for the fruit.

ANNIE WOODFORD

ACCUMULATION

It's cold. And while I'm better at frying chicken thighs
so the skin and rosemary stick,

I still haven't bought envelopes for these postage stamps,
or checked the mail for that package you sent.

I speculate it's a waffle iron,
but I've been wrong before.

■ ■ ■

It seems that, at my most creative,
I am finding ways not to love you.

I wonder, if we went ice-skating, and purpled our heels,
    would I pray
for a power line to fall, and buckle us like fainting goats?

■ ■ ■

There was a blizzard in Knoxville, the day I called
to pay off my court fines. It's forty

here, in northern Ohio, and the snow mortars
weeping pillboxes in the Kroger parking lot

where dejected Samoans
joist themselves with canvas crack-straps,

flaring in cart-wrangler Day-Glo vests—this
is what I'll return to—

ducking the plastic breezeway strips,
banging around in a corral.

■ ■ ■

Even in late January, the boxer
on Prospect worries a punching bag in his yard.

Its dry thud, like the sudden moment of inspiration
when a frozen lake decides to split.

LUKE MARINAC

THE DOG WARMS ONE OF MY BLUE FEET

extending beyond the edge of a pin-stripe
and polka-dot quilted Appalachia, where

voices lope like pickup cams, come unbolted and
    jettisoned
over hollers, to lie forgotten and bursting into Kudzu.

Like a muddy river, Tennessee crooks one arm over
Knoxville's thin and weather-beaten shoulders,

like my shoulders, indecipherable from a clothes hanger, or
the way the Midwest goes to its morning gothic

with a stiff purpose; a sports coat, and the hearse-like
    austerity
only a warm garment bag can lend.

LUKE MARINAC

PLANNED DEVELOPMENT

STEPHEN BROWN

Jack Hodges ignored the mechanical voice of the GPS urging him to turn around. The roads didn't exist yet, but he recognized the stand of redbud trees. He had played here as a child every Sunday after church while his parents enjoyed their weekly picnic.

He followed two meandering ruts cut into the reddish-clay soil. Tall dropseed grass scraped against the bottom of his truck, and his approach flushed a covey of Northern Bobwhite quail who were feeding on the seeds. A red-tailed hawk soared into view, tracking their retreat through the tall stalks.

The truck tires kicked up pieces of gravel and sent them pinging against the fenders when he crossed the wash where blackberries grew so thick you could eat your fill and still carry home five-gallon buckets full for pies or cobbler.

A swarm of honey bees were working the clump of giant blue hyssop near the top of the rise. He rolled down his window, heard them buzzing around the lavender stalks as he drove past. Switch grass and fox sedge had reclaimed the ruts on the far side of the wash. The slender stalks were heavy with seed and swayed in the light breeze as the cool morning air sank deeper into the canyon. He had ridden his bicycle along every animal trail that meandered through this entire grassland. Little green plastic flags marking the golf course fluttered alongside the tall stems of the native grasses.

Most people turned around at the wash, so the track on this side was little more than two vaguely marked lines of matted grasses. Faint indentations meandered around a limestone outcropping where water collected after it rained. A black phoebe called to its mate from one of the small puddles atop the limestone shelf. *Fee-bee, fee-bee* it trilled, its call the same as its name.

Jack parked on the southwest side of a persimmon tree where afternoon shade would keep the truck's interior cool. He looked up and studied the lowest branches: the fruit hanging above the cab wouldn't be ripe enough to drop for another month—no danger of dents or a broken windshield until then. The truck was new enough that he was still making payments. The low-boy trailer he was pulling was starting to show its age. He'd have to replace it soon. Thank God the dozer was paid for.

This is where he had brought Tracy for their first kiss. Hell, their first child had been conceived beneath the same tree. A bushy viburnum grew near a small seep. The blossoms smelled a little like some of that fancy perfume Tracy wore for special occasions, like when they went out to dinner to celebrate their anniversary.

He climbed down from the cab of his truck. The sound of his door slamming shut spooked a doe with a fawn young enough to still have spots. The deer stepped into a grove of river birch and blended into the shadows—perfectly camouflaged among the snowy-white trunks and brown strips of peeling bark.

The sun glinted off something shiny near a cluster of wild sage where they had been feeding, so he strolled over to have a look, picked up a candy wrapper, folded it clean-side out and stuffed it in a pocket. Breaking off a twig from the nearest sage, he stripped the leaves from the square stalk with

The sound of his door slamming shut spooked a doe with a fawn young enough to still have spots.

his thumb and index finger. He rubbed his palms together to crush the leaves and release the fragrant scent, tucking the twig into his pocket for later.

He checked his watch; he was early. Enough time to hike up to Lookout Point. This is where he'd come with his son the last time they'd ever talked, the day before Francis shipped out to Afghanistan and never came back. Three generations of family footprints had formed a rocky path toward the highest point. A low-hanging branch from a hazelnut was stripped of leaves and missing some of its bark where the trail was steepest. He grabbed hold of the slender branch and used it as a rope to pull himself up to the nearest foothold. The granite outcropping above his head was worn smooth from the number of hands that had wrapped their fingers around the knurled edges for support. A small cleft was just wide enough to step on. This was the tricky part. He had to let go of one thing to grab onto a higher one, but it had always been there. One more step, a slight reach...got it.

The view from the top of the hill was worth the climb. His house was two blocks over from the water tower that looked like a space ship. A tug boat steamed upriver, pushing a mountain of coal toward the power plant. It was all visible from here, two weeks of work. Yellow for sewage, red for power, and orange for cable, multi-hued strands of little plastic flags marked off where the trenches would go. All of the utilities would be underground to preserve the sightlines, but there wouldn't be anything left to see by the time all the houses were built. He headed back. It was much faster coming down.

Eight o'clock. Time for work. He hesitated. Took a deep breath. Turned the key. The diesel engine clattered to life with a billowing cloud of black smoke. He shifted into reverse and backed off the trailer. The metal tracks clanked down the ramps and bit into the soil, uprooting clumps of river oats and broad leaf sedge. He squinted into the sun. He blinked. Squeezed his eyes shut but it didn't help. A tear seeped loose from each eye and filled the tiny lines in his face, the wrinkles he'd collected from a lifetime spent outdoors. Jack cursed, but lowered the blade and began uprooting the plants they were naming the streets after. ■

DEEP SKY

how inappropriate the night
with all her gowning and un-gowning
when turns the day
she sheds her mantle
and teases sensuous light
with her long tendrils, raking them
across earth's belly, shudder
of wind, colder than
our mottled dead, blows along
river's edge, making it necessary
for night to re-don her dress

she grows impatient for her
daily illuminance
disappearing among the weeds
counting clouds
from earth's deep carpet
holding everything
in its vastness

KEVIN D. LEMASTER

A NATURAL AMERICAN

MICAH McCRARY

My very first car had a manual transmission: it was a red '91 Jeep Cherokee, which my father and I purchased together when I was twenty. It took a couple of weeks for me to get used to driving a stick shift, for me not to stall at an intersection or when pulling out of the driveway, but after I got the hang of it I came to love that car. I loved driving it around town, whether to class or to nowhere, and it not only felt like my car because I was its owner, but also because I felt I had so much control over it as a car with a manual transmission. And although I'd borrowed and driven my parents' cars before, my Jeep was the car that made me enjoy driving.

I'd been resistant to driving beforehand, whether in high school, when taking driving lessons from my parents (though mostly from my father), or after I got my license, when I could borrow a car for an errand, for work, or for school. My resistance in high school came from my father and I having always argued during my lessons—which frustrated me, making me want to give up on the idea of driving altogether. I hated my father's critiques. I hated the fact that there was always something to be said about what I did in the car, about this turn or that stop, and many times I told myself I'd rather just ride my bike or the town bus instead, because driving the way my father wanted me to was too difficult.

My mother wanted my father to give me most of my driving lessons, I'm guessing because she trusted him as a driver more than she trusted herself. My father holds a commercial driver's license, a CDL—he was once a semi-truck driver, and, once upon a time, was a taxi driver in Chicago. He'd had a lot of driving experience. He was a man who knew things about the road. He would teach me to drive in a way my mother couldn't.

Another part of my resistance to driving comes from knowing that when I'm in a car with an automatic transmission it feels too passive to me. Take this not as a warning that I'm zoning out on the road—it's just that, mechanically, I prefer my total engagement with the road to be paired with my total engagement with the car. I enjoy the sensation of the clutch. I like paying attention to my gears. This is the only way I take joy in driving.

When I drive my parents' cars during summers when I visit them—not owning a car where I currently live in southeastern Ohio and having moved there from Chicago—I find myself having to adjust to their cars in multiple ways. The first is that driving a car doesn't fit with the metaphor about remembering how to ride a bike—it may be easier to just get on a bike and go after you've been away from one for a while, but with a car it might be best to take it easy before getting into traffic.

The second adjustment is having to remember that I don't need to use both my left foot and my right hand to drive. This is odd for me because, even though I haven't driven the Jeep in ages, I should still know how to drive an automatic.

Because fewer cars now come with manual transmissions, I wonder whether I'll ever be be a happy driver. Like many people I've spent much of my life as a passenger, riding in cars first with my parents and then with my friends and then, after moving to Chicago, using public transportation, which I've come to prefer to getting behind the wheel any day. And having studied abroad a couple times, I'm also often nostalgic for the easiness of walking in European cities, wishing that more American cities possessed a topography built for the stroll.

As much as I'm thinking about driving here I'm also thinking about its alternatives, because I've learned as I've gotten older just how much I prefer being a passenger, even how much I prefer to walk or ride a bike. I'm brought here to think here about my old Jeep as a lost love: I've found myself now having to navigate less magical alternatives, a little bit persnickety about the ways I enjoy getting around.

■ ■ ■

I've been living in Athens, in Appalachian Ohio, for a little over two years, and I have zero complaints about what I see when I exit my front door, or when I walk from my house to my university's campus. While I do consider how much more convenient things might be if I *did* own a car (Athens is a considerably small town, just ten-and-a-half square miles in total area), the scenery is easier to take in when on foot, moving slower than when in a car and seeing the hills in the distance as still images rather than ones whizzing by.

Ohio, at least from what I've heard, has held a reputation for being "quintessentially American." While it might not have bits of vastly different cultures in it the way New York City or California do, much of its land has remained untouched. Its people enjoy their locales, frequenting the same paths on daily walks or bike rides, frequenting the same pubs

I've found myself now having to navigate less magical alternatives, a little bit persnickety about the ways I enjoy getting around.

during nightly outings. There was one night when two older gentlemen sitting beside a professor and myself at a bar cordially introduced themselves, gave us a drink they didn't want to finish, then left after taking a couple shots. "Welcome to Athens," my professor said, and I responded merely that I could get used to this.

"Quintessential Americanness," at least in the definition I'm looking for here, might include a neighborly friendliness, an appreciation for the place where one lives, and a willingness not to glamorize it at all. "There isn't much here," many Ohioans I've met have said to me about this place, but their tone is far from debilitated. They're happy with "not having much," however they might define *much*, and no one talks about their dreams of living in faraway places.

It gives me the impression that I've begun to think of this place, to a degree, as a kind of utopia: Not one where everyone around is made richer by the economic prospects here, but one where residents find bliss within this geography. When my professor gave me a breakdown of Athens, he said that many people have stuck around after finishing school to open businesses just for the sake of sticking around. "It's really nice to be in a place where people don't want to leave," he said, and I understood this feeling with clarity.

I've told a few friends about the ways this place reminds me of Prague, in the Czech Republic. While walking around Athens won't give me the sight of any thousand-year-old buildings, I'm reminded of Prague by the streets made of bricks instead of asphalt, by its river, by my ability to walk everywhere. Prague itself is a city on a hill, and Athens is a town within many hills, and it's been pleasant to walk both up- and downhill here, knowing that I'm not scanning for skyscrapers but rather for picturesque peaks.

But to compare this place (which is ostensibly American) with a city in Europe feels odd at best, and offensive at worst. I'm glad to be in a place again where I'm forced to walk so much, given a break from driving, because driving and the *necessity* of driving remind me that I'm in America. We love our cars and our open roads here, and we love to drive around, but there's something about now being in Ohio that feels strange—perhaps the actual strangeness isn't the place I've found myself in, but that it's me who ended up here.

■ ■ ■

I once read somewhere that Susan Sontag liked to call herself a "natural European." This is a complicated sentiment, for sure, in part because it can bring into question what makes a "natural American." Sontag *was* American, she was raised and befriended and educated by Americans, yet she found herself unwilling to define herself by an American patriotism.

I joke when in Prague about Czechs possessing a "beer belly patriotism," that one can't be a good Czech without appreciating beer and greasy food, but this phrase also makes me think of things like the NASCAR subculture in certain pockets of America, and the idea that one can, if they wish, define their Americanness through a love of leisure.

I sometimes want to side with Sontag by also calling myself a "natural European," but when I say this I have to place the qualities of my own character into two separate columns. *Natural* evokes the things that are already part of my preference and temperament—my dislike of driving, my dislike of guns, my love of wine at any time during the day—and shows me that many of the things I favor aren't characteristically American ones. In Europe it's easy to look down on things like binge-drinking or gun cultures, or even things like Hollywood, but in the U.S. it feels like making a list of the things I don't like is a kind of self-imposed exile, wherein the popular response to my list would be something like "If you don't like it here, then leave."

■ ■ ■

One night in Athens, on a walk home with a roommate, I told her about how romantic I am with real estate, always looking at homes and imagining myself in them. "Do you have a dream home?" she asked me, and I told her I hadn't figured that out yet. But I now think this may have been a lie. I've lived in many apartments, in part to rail against my parents' love of big houses, and I've romanticized these apartments because something about their comparatively small size has felt cozy to me. I've lived in four-bedrooms, in two-bedrooms, in studios, living in a townhouse is still on my to-do list, and I imagine a small cottage as being perfect. But real estate is not a buffet, I realize, and I have a feeling that the sampling I've done has just been one way of railing against an American pride in homeownership.

I've probably felt the same way about cars, having enjoyed my years in Chicago without one, even if owning a car might have made it easier to see friends in different neighborhoods or shop for groceries. My using the train there was both resistance and indulgence, reminding me that, it's possible for me to be quite a happy commuter in the U.S.

I love public transit, in fact. I love every city in the U.S. and elsewhere with a subway system. I love streetcars the most. And I've thought that being a passenger is far from a bad way to live, and that maybe it's this above all things that could

Living in Athens has made me wonder what it means to resist the U.S. while loving it at the same time.

make me a "natural European" like Sontag—Americans like driving because they like ownership, control, and freedom, but I myself feel more free when I'm being carried. I feel more free to read, to listen to music, to stare off into space, and the contradiction in my freedom here might be an inquiry of its own: Is my "passengerness" a kind of leisure, which is an American enjoyment, or is it a resistance to my American living?

Living in Athens has made me wonder what it means to resist the U.S. while loving it at the same time. The summers here are an ensemble of American experiences, from regular barbeques to celebrating the Fourth of July, and I appreciate the fun in all of this. This has also made me see, though, that maybe the benefit of European cities is that their distance from American ones allow for a distance from American experiences, from American habits.

■■■

One of my favorite essays is E.B. White's "Farewell, My Lovely" (originally published as "Farewell to the Model T"), in which White shows off not just his love for the Model T, but also the meaning it held for other people who drove one. It was a customizable (even if dangerous) car, and one could feel proud of the fact that their Model T could get a signature look by way of customization: A way of assuring others on the street that no one else could have a Model T like theirs.

White's essay, when I first came across it, reminded me of my Jeep, even though it was nowhere near as customizable, nowhere near being able to make it as mine as those old Model Ts were. But I understood why White was happy to own such a thing: It was the car that changed America, and to own one was to feel like you were a part of something American—just as for many today, to own a car, period, feels like "doing your part" in being an American. There's something off-putting about it for me, though—maybe it's the idea of car loans and car payments, or the insurance, or the maintenance, or the obvious class distinction that owning a car can hold, that has made me put off owning another one for so long.

To say that to own a car is to make one more American is unfair, especially to those in places where owning a car isn't necessary: like Athens, or like any of the numerous cities in the U.S. where it's possible to ride a streetcar or the subway.

Maybe because I grew up in a rural town and am now in rural Appalachia, or maybe because I got to taste for so long what it means to be separate from car culture, I've had trouble resolving my feelings toward once again living in a place that *has* a car culture. What maybe needs to be resolved here, what needs to be reconciled, is how to cope with once again living in a place where a car can feel like a luxury instead of a necessity.

What is there to do, then, in a place like Athens, to feel like I'm experiencing the town the "Athenian" (i.e. local/American/Appalachian) way? How can I maintain a naturalness here without giving in to the luxuries within reach? Is it possible that, if my immediate thoughts in Athens can be about hills and trees instead of about cars, I've found myself in my ideal geographic bubble? Is it possible that I've found myself in a place where, whether I'm being snobby about it or not, I'm not required to question my Americanness? ■

KEEPSAKE

On the famous path by the river,
I stoop and pick up a Buckeye
to keep in my pocket.

It is mine this river as it flows past
your house which is also mine, flows
past

its banks of paw paws
and cowcumber trees, with their nodding
saucer leaves.

The river's riffles
froth by the shoal before they run
full out, gurgling their

pebbly songs. You have
taken the tune out of them and gone.
I have this Buckeye.

NOEL SMITH

NO ANIMAL AFTERLIFE

See how wholly they open to us
in death, to the moon, to the red elm
scabbed with mites.
—*Bruce Snider*

Of course you are imagining an afterlife
for roadkill, but have you ever slowed
or even stopped to look closely
at a raccoon's teeth buried in tar to the gums?
See skunk smear near mustard flowers
where carrion birds dragged it—
black and white fur like silk in moonlight.

Either way, let me tell you about backyard-kill.
My brother and I loved to pour bleach on lizards.
It didn't always kill them; that wasn't our mission.
We enjoyed poking the billowed throats
of frogs to see if they'd pop
like a balloon. They never did.

We used to go on picnics near Big Devil's Fork Creek.
I saw a warthog near a turn-off, bristly black
and blood-wet around its snout. I said a prayer.
We'd bring our food and blanket to the edge
of the woods, and we'd walk to the granite outcrop
where "The Big Piney plummets into Dismal Creek,"
my father said. And he told about the large hole

the creek had bored through the bluff.
Instead of a waterfall, you see this detour
where water and its cargo of rocks

had broken through sandstone.
My father's last few words trailed off, because
my brother and I were watching a fox and a deer
drinking from the creek at the same time.

CHARLES CANTRELL

UP ON THE RIDGE

CHARLES WRIGHT'S CHILDHOOD HOME IN KINGSPORT, TENNESSEE

SCOTT HONEYCUTT

Rising above the city of Kingsport, Tennessee, Chestnut Street provides some of the finest winter views in all of Sullivan County. Old Stage Road belts across the top of the ridgeline, and to the north Clinch Mountain dominates the scene as it hangs over a valley peppered with outlines of farmsteads, church steeples and shops, and the ever-present billow of Tennessee Eastman's chemical plant. On the other side of the road, looking south toward Washington County, the scene drops into an undulated map of brown hills, interrupted with neighborhoods and fields. In the distance, back walls of the Blue Ridge stand up and highlight familiar profiles of Holston and the Iron Mountains along with the high knob of Roan Mountain, fading deep against the horizon. It is a beautiful place, and driving along the ridgetop it is easy to understand how such a scene could infuse itself into one's personal geography, locking down the landscape for a lifetime. As I drove along Old Stage Road in December of 2014, I was searching for more than views, I was hunting down memories; however these were not my own recollections, but the memories of another, a renowned writer who grew up along this lane seventy years ago.

The former United States Poet Laureate Charles Wright's early years are well documented. He was born in Pickwick Dam, Tennessee, on August 25th, 1935. His father, Charles Penzel Wright (1904-1972) was a civil engineer who worked on a variety of construction projects for TVA and was even employed on the Manhattan Project in Oak Ridge during the early 1940s. By the end of World War II, the 40-year-old elder Wright would relocate his family east to the bustling town of Kingsport. There he took employment with Eastman Chemical Company and would later operate his own small construction firm. Along with his wife, Mary Winter Wright (1910-1964), he would raise three children: eldest son Charles, known at the time as Chuck, middle son Winter, and a daughter named Hildegard (1941-1991). Chuck would attend Kingsport's Lincoln Elementary before he was sent to private religious schools in the North Carolina mountains. After high school, Wright attended Davidson College, north of Charlotte, earning a history degree in 1957. According to Wright, however, he did not begin to compose verse until 1959 when he was stationed with an Army Intelligence unit in Verona, Italy. "I found the lyric poem," Wright explains in a 2005 interview, "I was reading the selected poems of Ezra Pound, and I found a poem about the place where I was, Lake Garda, Sermione Peninsula."[1] He expands:

> *I started writing in Italy when I was in the Army because I was taken by what I was seeing; it was so different from what I was used to seeing in Appalachia—east Tennessee and western North Carolina where I grew up. Then for several years I wrote out of that experience; and then suddenly one day I realized that I had a past and a childhood, and it all came sort of flowing into me, through me, and out of me, I guess [...] It brought back the landscapes of my childhood.*[2]

Throughout his long career, Wright's poems have probed and illuminated the multiple landscapes of lived experience: from the Italian countryside to the blue California coastline and from a summer home in Montana to his own backyard in Charlottesville, Virginia. However, for me, Wright's most

Wright's poems have probed and illuminated the multiple landscapes of lived experience...

poignant poems are the ones that are set among the landscapes of his childhood in Kingsport, those Appalachian snapshots of a time long past but still quite accessible in the present. Critics have noted how autobiographical landscapes would come to play a central role in forming his canon. One of Wright's first ventures into these autobiographic tropes appeared the 1973 poem "Dog Creek Mainline." This poem captures imagistic shards of memory arising from his youngest recollections while living in Hiawassee Village, North Carolina. Wright has admitted, "that a shift occurred" with the publication of "Dog Creek Mainline." "Suddenly," he told interviewer David Skeel, "I realized that for once in his life Rilke was right. Every writer has a subject matter: his own life."[3]

For readers from Appalachia, Wright's poems intrigue because he carries our familiar place names and terrains with him on his quest for poetic transcendence. As a result, even little Kingsport, Tennessee, can swim in the same waters as Verona, Italy. Wright has been called a poetic pilgrim who long ago set out on what scholar Robert Denham calls "a variation of the quest romance."[4] For Wright, "Poems are not just about journeys, of course, they are journeys."[5] Though he has traveled long and far from his beginnings in Kingsport, every pilgrim must have a starting place, a departing coastline, and no matter how far he has journeyed, there seems to be no escaping the gravity of his homeland. In the wonderfully titled "All Landscape is Abstract, and Tends to Repeat Itself," Wright acknowledges his permanent bond with the region: "Over the Blue Ridge, the whisperer starts to whisper in tongues / Remembered landscapes are left in me / The way a bee leaves its sting, /hopelessly, passion-placed, / Untranslatable language / [...] All forms of landscape are autobiographical.[6]

1 W.T. Pfefferle. "Charles Wright: Charlottesville, Virginia." *Poets on Place: Interviews and Tales from the Road* (Logan: Utah State University Press, 2005), 191.

2 Ibid., 190.

3 David Skeel. "Captain Dog: A Conversation with Charles Wright." *Books and Culture: A Christian Review* 16, no.2 (March-April 2010): 16.

4 Robert D. Denham. *Charles Wright: A Companion to the Late Poetry, 1988-2007* (Jefferson, NC, and London: McFarland and Co., 2008), 11.

5 Ibid.

6 Charles Wright. "All Landscape is Abstract and Tends to Repeat Itself." *Negative Blue: Selected Later Poems* (New York: Farrar, Straus and Giroux, 2000), 158.

In his preface to *Charles Wright: A Companion to the Late Poetry, 1988-2007,* Denham notes that "there is widespread agreement that Wright's place in the pantheon of American poets is assured." He goes on to evince that "there have been more than 130 essays and articles about his work [and] there are more than 170 reviews of [Wright's poetry] [...] but for all this attention, no one has attempted a book-length study of his work."[7] I will add to Denham's observations and state that while many apt writers have commented on Wright's challenging verse, no one as yet has thoroughly and physically probed the actual Tennessee landscapes that implicitly and quite often explicitly haunt so much his work. I'm unaware of any critics who have actually completed their own pilgrimages up the ridge to walk the grounds where, to use Wright's own words, he "really grew up."[8]

When I pulled into the driveway, I noticed that the owners were keeping the old homestead in top form. Though winter, the grass was well-groomed and the exterior was trimmed in reds and greens of the Christmas season; the house, a whitewashed brick rancher was constructed in the early 1940s. It looked cozy yet solid. As I stepped out of my truck and headed up the sidewalk, I was reminded of Wright's 2007 book-length poem entitled *Littlefoot,* which begins:

It may not be written in any book, but it is written –
You can't go back,
                    You can't repeat the unrepeatable.
No matter how fast you drive, or how hard the slide show
Of memory flicks and releases,
It's always some other place,
                    Some other car in the driveway,
Someone unrecognizable about to open door.[9]

On this day, the unrecognizable car was a late model mini-van and that unrecognizable person who opened the door was the home's current owner, a woman named Sandy. She greeted me with a warm "hello" as she welcomed me in her own home, not Charles Wright's. She and her family had lived there for over ten years, and before they moved in, Sandy's father in-law, Dick, had owned the property for more than a decade. In the late 1990s, Dick had met the poet's brother, when Winter had traveled up from Savannah, Georgia, to show his wife the ridge. Since that time, no strangers had come asking to tour the house, so it had drifted back into the everyday world of private life. Sandy confessed that she was not familiar with Wright's work and that she did not even know her house had a literary heritage until the summer when the *Kingsport Times* ran an article highlighting Wright's appointment as poet laureate. It seems that I was to be the home's first literary investigator.

What struck me most about the house was its size. From the outside, it looks quite modest, but the interior reveals a spacious and curious design that winds to over 2,600 square feet on two levels. Sandy led me into the living room where we sat and talked about the home's remodeling projects and additions made throughout the years. I was particularly intrigued with how the front door had been relocated down toward the carport. Originally, it was positioned beside the chimney, but now that space is occupied by large bay windows. Sandy suspected that the door was moved because of its proximity to the hearth and chimney; perhaps too much heat

7 Denham, 1.

8 David Cross Turner. "Oblivion's Glow: The (Post) Southern Sides of Charles Wright." *storySouth* Summer 2005. Rpt. In Denham, 146.

9 Charles Wright. *Littlefoot. Bye-and-Bye: Selected Late Poems* (New York: Farrar, Straus and Giroux, 2011), 203.

escaped in winter months. Another curiosity: though the hard wood floors have been repaneled, there is one remaining strip of the original heart-of-pine; it runs perpendicular with the rest of the grain as it cuts an obvious swath through the front center of the living room. The dark floor panel stretches out like a fixed shadow; it's a fitting symbol for the poet's work—the past lingering like scar tissue.

Adjacent to the living room was a darkened master suite. I imagine it was Wright's parents' bedroom because it is the largest in the house and still holds an air of authority. Next, Sandy led me through the brightly lit kitchen and dining room where she pointed out changes they had made in paint coloring and flooring. At last we stepped over into the back hallway, and here came to the stairwell that descended into a labyrinthine

The germ for Wright's entire catalog is contained within the pictures boundaries: the past, landscape, family, and home...

basement. Full of mysterious nooks and narrow passageways, the finished bottom floor twists and intersects from room to room.

In this basement, just below the stairs, hangs a framed poster of Sandy's husband's favorite blues rock musician—the late Johnny Winter. This poster is highly coincidental because Johnny and his brother Edgar—another fine musician—are first cousins to Charles Wright. The brothers grew up in Beaumont, Texas, sons of Mary Winter Wright's brother. There are reports of them visiting Kingsport during the 1950s. In the summer of 2014, one local resident wrote to the *Kingsport Times*, and recollected the brothers' visit: "I grew up on Old Stage Road next door to the Wright family. I was born in 1949 so the Wright children were a lot older. I vaguely remember, when I was very young, that two albino boys would come visit the Wrights."[10] Seeing Johnny Winter's face was a revelation, especially since neither Sandy nor her husband had ever read any of Wright's own verse, nor were they aware of the familial relation. It seems the family's connections just seeped into the house.

Directly to the left of Winter's poster and down a short hallway is a rectangular-shaped bedroom tucked under a low hanging ceiling. I later confirmed that this was once the poet's bedroom. Sandy's son also grew up in here, and now that he is enlisted in the military it has been transformed into a shrine for the Marine Corps. Dark red, almost maroon, paint swashes the room and large letters U.S.M.C. emblazon across the wall above the bed. While I was admiring the bedroom and imagining the child-Wright occupying this place so many years before, Sandy handed me a photo of the poet taken in the late 1940s. To be more precise, it is a photo of Charles, Sr. In it, he stands at attention, dark eyes facing straight ahead and one hand in his pocket. It may have been taken in the early spring because the trees have not leafed out yet. Standing in the background two girls wave at the camera, and in the right hand corner, the young poet steps into the frame: he's twelve years old, his denim pants are rounded up and his left hand dives into a pocket, intimating his father's gesture. Unlike his father, though, who gazes stoically into the camera, young Chuck seems to be casting a slight smile upward as the moment catches his movement through the space. The germ for Wright's entire catalog is contained within the picture's boundaries: the past, landscape, family, and home, all encapsulated in this one instant.

10 Vince Staten. "Charles Wright." 24 June 2014. E-mail.

Though it has been many years since Wright's family has lived on Old Stage Road, it is not difficult to imagine the home as the poet experienced it. Enough of his work directly refers back to this ridge that his presence remains palpable. For example, in Wright's 1981 poem "The Southern Cross" his speaker cedes to the fallibility of memory but simultaneously notes how past places, though forgotten, shape who we grow to become. He observes, "It's what we forget that defines us, and stays in the same place / and waits to be rediscovered."[11] Earlier in "The Southern Cross," the speaker recalls leaving the very room where I was now standing:

> *I can't remember enough.*
> *How the hills, for instance, at dawn in Kingsport*
> *In late December in 1962 were black*
> *against the sky.*
> *The color of pale fish blood and water that ran to white*
> *As I got ready to leave home for the hundredth time,*
> *My mother and father asleep,*
> *My sister asleep,*
> *Carter's Valley as dark as the inside of a bone*
> *Below the ridge,*
> *the first knobs of the Great Smokies*
> *Beginning to stick through the sunrise" (my emphasis).*[12]

The childhood recollections that the poet/speaker weaves throughout his work could be viewed as every day and even ordinary, yet his work cuts against those stereotypical agrarian poetics found throughout Appalachian verse: he presents a decidedly middle-class voice, even, perhaps, a privileged one. Certainly poets from Appalachia are famed for their sense of place, ties to the land and extricable, familiar memories. Wright's poetry, however, expands our definitions of

Appalachia poetic sensibility. Wright's father was not a farmer, so in his work, descriptions of the ridgetop view will often intermingle with more suburban landmarks: the public spaces of drug stores, civic auditoriums, schools house, Highway 11E, and even hot rods stream fluidly throughout his catalog. In this manner, Wright's Kingsport poems function as civic as well as private memory. They present and preserve the world of a mid-century Appalachian town, moving away from pastoral ambition into an industrial one. Over the years, I have talked with several long time Kingsport residents, and they often reply after reading Wright's poetry, "Yes, I remember those places. I was there too, years ago, though I recall them a little differently."

Even though the city of Kingsport has enlarged since Wright's childhood, the road along Chestnut Ridge has not changed much over the years. Geography dictates this stasis; it is too narrow for broad development. Of course, more homes line the ridge now than in years past, and of course the gravel has been replaced with blacktop, but for all this change, the alterations seem largely superficial. Photos from the time period illustrate that Wright's childhood terrain possessed a rural environment that was drifting into a suburban one. The lot across from his home was seeded with corn, and fields skid down from either side of the lane, but all along the road houses were beginning to be constructed and whole neighborhoods were encroaching. Fortunately, straight across from the house there remains one of the last undeveloped lots along Old Stage Road; now, instead of being planted in corn, it flourishes as an overgrown bramble of privet and blackberry vines, but the

11 Charles Wright. "The Southern Cross." *The World of the Ten Thousand Things 1980-1990* (New York: Farrar, Straus, and Giroux, 1990), 54.

12 Ibid., 52-53.

view of Clinch Mountain remains intact. Here, even location names evoke nostalgic and poetry—Old Stage Road, a traveler's highway from by-gone years and Chestnut Ridge, an elegiac nod to the once dominant trees of the eastern forests, forever lost to the great blight.

On a north facing slope, directly across from the house, grows a stout cherry tree completely wrapped in English ivy. It is large enough to have been rising there since Wright's childhood. In fact, he may be alluding this particular tree in "Link Chain." Published in 1975, this work finds the speaker musing once again on Wright's perennial subjects: time and morality. The speaker confides, "I'd lay my body down, In Tennessee, / [...] I'd pick a tree, black cherry, / That grows on the north side of Chestnut Ridge, and looks out / Over the Cumberlands.[13]

Though Wright has cautioned that "my landscapes have always been imaginary, invented, and reconstructed," there is no denying the veracity of his verse to capture this specific vista and tangible place.[14] Consider how in Littlefoot he returns again to the ridge:

> *In Kingsport, looking across the valley toward Moccasin Gap*
> *From Chestnut Ridge,*
> *the winter-waxed trees*
> *Are twiggy and long-fingered, fretting the woods-wind,*
> *Whose songs, ghost songs, wind-lyrics from sixty years ago,*
> *Float back and exhale—*
> *I will twine with my mingles of raven black hair.*
> *Will you miss me when I'm gone?*[15]

The penultimate question that hangs in the ending lines serve as a refrain for the entirety of *Littlefoot: Will you miss me when I'm gone?* He asks over and over at the poem's conclusion.

These words echo those of the legendary country group, the Carter Family. It is no coincidence that Wright chooses the Carter Family's words to end his long meditation on family and impermanence. Chestnut Ridge peers out toward the landscapes of the Carter's old homestead in Maces Springs, Virginia, so his question poses a kind of metaphorical call and response across the valley, between the mountain and the ridge. Like barred owls calling back and forth in the night, they keep probing: *Will you miss me when I'm gone?* The only answer that comes to mind are five short words–yes, of course, we will. Again his implausible question, *"Will you miss me when I gone?"* Yes, of course, we answer but those us from Appalachia understand that you are never really gone, so long as Clinch Mountain looms over the valley, there will be memories worth sharing and songs worth singing.

The lonesome and plaintive mountain lyrics of *Littlefoot* would arise again in Wright's greatest tribute to his family's past. First published in 2000, "Appalachian Lullaby" was to be a kind of swan song to the ridge. At a reading in 2004, Wright stated "I promised myself it would be the last time that I would write about Appalachia, which I've spent forty years doing."[16] Though, inevitably, it is not the final time that he would gaze back over his youth, "Appalachian Lullaby," seamlessly captures an amalgamation of landscape and memory as it follows mortality's eraser, dropping down to bring a beautiful and absolute oblivion:

13 Charles Wright. "Link Chain." *Bloodlines* (Middletown: Wesleyan University Press, 1973), 73.

14 Charles Wright. *Halflife: Improvisations and Interviews, 1977-87* (Ann Arbor: University of Michigan Press, 1988), 181.

15 Wright, *Littlefoot*, 215.

16 Wright, Charles. "A Reading by Charles Wright." November 5, 2003. Virginia Museum of Fine Arts. *Blackbird* Archive. Department of English at Virginia Commonwealth University. Spring 2004, Vol. 3, 1.

In Kingsport, high on a ridge,
night is seeping out of the Cumberlands
And two-steps the hills, shadows in ecstasy across the sky–
Not dark, not dark, but almost,
deep and sweet repose[...]
My sister and mother and father, each
in a separate room,
stay locked in a private music and drift away, night
And day, drift way [...]
Time, slow liquid, like a black highway in front of me [...]
Hello goodbye hello. Works and days.
We come, we hang out, we disappear.
There are stars that can't be counted,
and can't be counted on.
Gently the eyelids close.
Not dark, not dark. But almost.
Drift away. And drift away.
A deep and sweet repose.[17]

So what does it all mean? Why is it enriching to visit Wright's ridge, to kick through the dust of another's past? I suppose this question could be leveled at any number of literary places that form our culture's secular shrines. From the high temple of Henry David Thoreau's Walden Pond to more regional attractions like Thomas Wolfe's boardinghouse in Asheville, these landmarks function as sources of national and regional pride as they confirm the notion that one among us had some something artful and powerful to say about a place, and that we, too, though separated by time and experience, can dip into their world as they dip into ours, as they imprint their own private landscape across our memoires, connecting the past with the future and helping us to transcend the brevity of our own lives. I think too often when we consider poetry, if we consider it at all, we perceive it as somehow distant and too abstract an art form, so we believe it takes place beyond our understanding. Yet to read Charles Wright's poetry and then to drive along Old Stage Road in the winter months when the leaves are down, is to read our own world, and see our everyday lives here in the Tri-Cities as wondrous and mysterious as any place on the globe.

The long shadows of winter punctured the air as I returned to my truck. I backed out of the drive way and then began the short drive that wound down the ridge. To the south, Roan Mountain stood, a dark smudge along horizon and to the north, Moccasin Gap leaned into Virginia, both as timeless as the earth and both as lovely as poems. ■

17 Charles Wright. "Appalachian Lullaby." *Bye-and-Bye: Selected Late Poems* (New York: Farrar, Straus and Giroux, 2011)36-37.

AVIARY

After Tim Barnwell's photograph, "Emma Mills on porch with chickens, 1982"

I don't much care what they'll think,
folks who'll see this photograph
hung in Tim's shop window,
what they'll assume about my life
in Dry Branch. When they see
the hollows in my face, thin ropes
of my arms, they'll see a type,
I guess, woman bent against
mountain with few means to leave.
But I am here of my own
accord, free as these chickens
scuffling for split corn spilled
on the porch. They're not caged
or clipped but hop and hitch there
by the Sealtest crate, small gleaners
oblivious to their fate.

PHILIP BELCHER

BOOK REVIEW

Connie May Fowler. *A Million Fragile Bones*. Tallahassee, Fl.: Twisted Road Publications, 2017. 320 pages. Softcover. $15.95.

Reviewed by Katherine Scott Crawford

Connie May Fowler's environmental memoir *A Million Fragile Bones* does not promise to make you fall in love, and then break your heart—but it does both.

Set on Alligator Point, a tiny sandbar on Florida's northern Gulf coast, the memoir is a chronicle of Fowler's life against the backdrop of the 2010 Deepwater Horizon explosion and its aftermath. Its opening chapters, however, exist in the time before the spill, as Fowler works through the effects of an abusive childhood and the loss of her father. She heals herself—or, more aptly, would insist that Alligator

Point healed her—by engaging in a total immersion in the surrounding natural world. Her days are marked by life in and around her self-designated "shack" on the Point: by the tides, the weather, the migration patterns of Monarchs, the movement of sand and sea creatures.

This is a world of near-to unutterable beauty. But Fowler, a writer never fearful of the deep, here goes wide-armed at the edge, welcoming the diver's plummet into detail. "The world glittered with critters on the wing," she writes, "the light deepening into a meditative fugue, and my inner landscape shifted: a spry spiritual realignment, a faint recognition of something ancient regained. It was as if old waters long hidden became tidal and known."

There are themes here, of course—about love, loss, family, shame, abuse, healing, reemergence, greed, warning and hope—and they are important. After you've fallen in love with Fowler's Florida—and you won't be able to help yourself, even knowing your history—it is still a surprise when, in the middle of the memoir, the Deepwater Horizon oil rig explodes in the Gulf of Mexico. It is still a surprise when BP struggles to control the aftershock of an estimated 4.9 million gallons of oil spewing into the Gulf. Despite our futuristic stance from 2017, the disaster and its aftermath is astonishing. This is because it's difficult to imagine that anything can destroy the world Fowler has illuminated.

Though it earns its unique designation as an "environmental memoir," *A Million Fragile Bones* is just as full of people and animals—Fowler's companions and friends—as it is of land, sea and sky. Fowler's beloved dogs, those she rescued and who rescued her, fill her shack with joy, and pepper the memoir with laugh-out-loud humor, despite its serious concerns. Fowler's husband, Bill, whom she meets and falls in love with during her time on the Point, gives her life there even more emotional heft: he is a steady, gifted partner, one Fowler seems to have earned after years of heartbreak and loss.

The devastation wreaked upon the environment after the Deepwater Horizon disaster, as with any disaster of this magnitude, was as difficult to grasp in 2010 as it is now. But by offering up the personal details of her world, Fowler gives readers an access to the destruction, and to her own grief and anger, which reverberates with intimacy. This can't be easy. But as Fowler says, "Writing is an act of courage by people who know if they don't tell their truths, their hearts will explode."

A Million Fragile Bones is a marriage of truth-telling and story: it is a love letter to the natural world, and a grief-stricken wail at its destruction, as the book jacket says, "for the sake of corporate profits." But it is her examination of the connection between humans and the natural world that keeps the book from sinking into sorrow. The composition Fowler creates from this connection—her exploration of our shared DNA— is nothing less than a love song of molecules. Because of this, her fury is righteous, and her pen is mighty.

Maurice Manning. *One Man's Dark*. Port Townsend, Wa.: Copper Canyon Press, 2016. 110 pages. Hardcover. $23.00.

Reviewed by John Lang

On the cover of *One Man's Dark*, Maurice Manning's superb new collection of poems, appears a sepia photograph of the interior of an empty tobacco barn, sunlight visible on and through the spaced boards of the barn's far wall. That photograph, like Manning's poems, reflects the rural Appalachian world in which this poet is grounded, the barn's emptiness indicative of the ongoing erosion of rural life, a recurring concern in Manning's often elegiac poetry. Yet the radiating light in the photo attests to the underlying optimism of his writing and to the celebratory, visionary impulse that pervades the book, a stance apparent in the volume's epigraph, a verse from the prophet Isaiah: "I will sing for my beloved my love-song about his vineyard." For Manning, that beloved is ultimately the Creator of nature, about whom he writes, "God gave us a green world", green being the dominant color throughout this collection, although Manning acknowledges, too, the "dimming green" that results from humanity's assault on nature. In the face of environmental destruction, *One Man's Dark* emphasizes human beings' dependence on both nature and the divine, and thus the book is filled with poignant descriptions of nature's beauty—especially that of woods, hills, rivers and streams, rain, and various birds—as well as with explicit references to God and to "wondering / about a world you cannot see", including "all the unseen underneath" natural phenomena.

According to Manning, *One Man's Dark* is the final volume of a trilogy that began with *The Common Man* (2010) and continued in *The Gone and the Going Away* (2013). The latter collection's concluding poem, "The Prayer," addresses God as "Lord of all greening, / Lord of night," while this new book's first poem, "The Pinch," opens with similar religious language:

> *Here in Kentucky, a world and, yet,*
> *a second, unknowable world are drawn*
> *almost together between God's thumb*
> *and famous, animating finger.*
> *It's a tight place, but I've seen it—*
> *believe me, I see it every day.*

The monosyllabic diction of this quotation's fifth line underscores the speaker's confidence in his experience of this liminal place that yokes seen and unseen, the natural and the supernatural, the knowable and the ineluctably mysterious. The flexible, unrhymed iambic tetrameter of these lines recurs throughout the book's forty-six poems and is perhaps Manning's favorite meter, one that he described in an interview published in the *Iron Mountain Review* as "more a measure of the way we speak now" than iambic pentameter. The pinch of this poem's title suggests complication or difficulty, but it also recalls the proverbial action that helps determine whether one is asleep or awake. In Manning's work, however, awakening often involves acquiring both a sense of wonder and, paradoxically, the capacity to dream. Many of the poems in this collection recount dreams or mention assorted dreams: "the dream to make the world whole / by my [the poet's] dream, and a dream before my own / remembered"; "a human dream of redemption"; and what the speaker of the book's final poem calls "my love-dream". In Manning's work the term "dream" denotes both the energy of the human imagination in its mythopoeic activity and the limitations of human reason, as when he writes, "but logic has an end—it ends / in the woods, it ends inside a dream". Human vision, he implies, must embrace the visionary if it is to begin to grasp the significance of the wonders amidst which people find themselves, for "the dream illuminates the real," just as fiction and poetry do. In the act of creation, God also dreams, perhaps the very "dream before my own" to which Manning refers, for he presents the woods as "God's idea, the living dream / with nothing as its precedent". This is Manning's version of creation ex nihilo.

Lest these remarks lead readers of this review to conclude, falsely, that *One Man's Dark* is all too mystical or ethereal,

I would hasten to assure those readers that the collection incorporates a wide range of poems, some of them primarily meditative and philosophical, others predominantly descriptive or narrative. Manning is a gifted storyteller who slights neither the physical world nor the metaphysical, yet who fills this book with a whimsical assortment of often-humorous characters, some of whose names clearly verge on the allegorical: Mister Key, Sylvanus Shade, Jonsee Ponder, Jonah Payne, Lucian ("Luce") Loving, along with Loving's antagonist, the demonic Elder Sinkhorn. In this connection, moreover, in the volume's sixth poem Manning mentions a book titled *Progress?*—the question mark challenging most Americans' assumption (at least till recently) about the inevitable course of history. This early use of the word "progress" also seems meant to allude to John Bunyan's famous allegory and to the poet's own pilgrimage, for in several of the poems the speaker is portrayed in motion, walking towards or into some new experience or revelation. One of the major challenges Manning sets himself is that of effectively articulating such moments of grace or of mystical communion, a challenge he successfully meets time and again in such poems as "Patch of Light in Deep Woods," "Obedience," "Stream at Night," and "Amid the Flood of Mortal Ills Prevailing," that last title a phrase from Martin Luther's great hymn "A Mighty Fortress."

Accompanying Maurice Manning through this collection is rewarding exercise indeed, whether he depicts a moment of illumination like that in "A Field of Tiger Lilies in Kentucky," or recounts the anguish of remorse in "Something to Say about Possums," or contemplates "the love beyond our love" in "The Woodcock," a species of love that another poem professes "shall reach beyond all reason, / beyond return and understanding". For Manning, "Faith and love are seeds to plant / in the mystery of Time", his capitalization of Time endowing it with an aura of the sacred and highlighting its identity as a divine gift. *One Man's Dark* is a major achievement, and Maurice Manning is a major American poet speaking from the heart of Appalachia. ■

PLAYING FOREVER

What comes over someone
that they can play and sing
and move from song to song
like walking from tree to tree
in a forest
            or room to room
in a big old house.

Someone asked me if I ever
ran out of songs.

There is always another song
though my fingers hurt
and the rocking chair
is more than a prop.

Always another song
another measure
another shift. I don't sing
much anymore. Mountains
don't end, they go on and on
until they flatten for a while
only to rise again.

But not play the same tune twice.
I'm not so sure about that.
Things come around again,
don't they? Just when you think
you've figured it out—
how not to gossip about your neighbors

or scratch that itch, how to live
without your mama—
it comes around. Songs are like that, too.
The old ones, the ones I love,
they harken to each other
a hammer on here, the frail there
in just the same way
as that song it seems I only just played.

But no, I don't think I'll
ever run out of songs.
Though it may be
that my hands will get too
tired to play them.

LORI GRAVLEY

CONTRIBUTORS

Joseph Bathanti is former Poet Laureate of North Carolina (2012-14) and recipient of the 2016 North Carolina Award for Literature. He is the author of ten books of poetry, including *The 13th Sunday after Pentecost,* released in 2016. Bathanti is Professor of Creative Writing at Appalachian State University in Boone, North Carolina, and the University's Watauga Residential College Writer-in-Residence.

Philip Belcher is the Vice President of Programs for The Community Foundation of Western North Carolina in Asheville and the author of a chapbook, *The Flies and Their Lovely Names.* Belcher's poems and prose have appeared in numerous journals, including *The Southeast Review, Shenandoah, Southern Humanities Review, Passages North, Fugue, The Southern Quarterly,* and Asheville Poetry Review. He is an Advisory and Contributing Editor for *Shenandoah.*

Stephen Brown is the author of *Shadows of Chaco Canyon,* an historical mystery novel. A National Park Service Albright-Wirth grant to research the Underground Railroad led to his second book: *A Promise Moon.* He is scheduled to graduate from Spalding University's MFA Program in November 2017 and his preliminary master's thesis has been accepted as an online resource by the University of New Mexico.

Charles Cantrell taught English for several years at Madison Area Technical College in Wisconsin. He has held numerous residencies at the Virginia Center for the Creative Art and Ragdale. The author of two chapbooks, *Cicatrix* and *Greatest Hits,* he has published poems in *Poetry Northwest, The Literary Review, Southern Poetry Review, Prairie Schooner,* and other publications.

Samantha Cole is a current resident of Berea, Kentucky, who grew up in Beattyville, Kentucky. She enjoys reading, and occasionally writes poetry or fiction about modern mountain life. She has been published in *Appalachian Heritage, Kudzu,* and *Still: The Journal.*

Katherine Scott Crawford is an award-winning writer, newspaper columnist, and college English teacher. Author of the historical novel *Keowee Valley*, her work has appeared in literary journals and magazines, including *South Loop Review, The Santa Fe Writer's Project,* and *Wilderness House Literary Review*. Crawford holds an MFA in Creative Writing from Vermont College of Fine Arts and lives in Western North Carolina with her husband and daughters.

Lori Gravley writes poetry, fiction, and creative nonfiction. She earned her MFA from the University of Texas at El Paso. She has published poems in a variety of journals, recently including *I-70 Review, Burningword,* and *Crack the Spine*. She travels the world for her work as a USAID consultant, but her home is in Yellow Springs, Ohio. You can hear her on Conrad's Corner and listen to her interviews with other poets at WYSO Public Radio.

Michael Gray received his MFA from Florida Atlantic University and currently serves as an Associate Professor of English at John Tyler Community College in Virginia. His fiction has appeared in *The Baltimore Review, Carte Blanche, Fiction Southeast,* and *Coe Review*.

Janet S. Holloway was born and raised in Logan County, West Virginia, and spent many summers on her grandmother's tobacco farm outside of Abingdon, Virginia. She's the author of *A Willful Child,* and her second memoir, *Leaving,* will be published in June. A graduate of Marshall University, Holloway lives in Lexington, Kentucky.

Scott Honeycutt grew up in Virginia and Tennessee. For many years, he taught high school English south of Atlanta before earning a Ph.D. in American literature from Georgia State University. He is an Assistant Professor of English at East Tennessee State University in Johnson City, Tennessee. When not teaching, Honeycutt enjoys walking the hills of Appalachia and spending time with his family.

Julia Campbell Johnson received an MFA in Creative Writing from American University. Her poems have appeared in *Potomac Review, Southern Poetry Review,* and *Poet Lore,* among others. Her chapbook, *The Tea of the Unforeseen Berry,* was published by Finishing Line Press. She is a Fellow of the Virginia Center for the Creative Arts.

John Lang is the author of *Understanding Fred Chappell, Six Poets from the Mountain South*, and most recently, *Understanding Ron Rash*. A Professor of English Emeritus at Emory & Henry College, where he taught from 1983 to 2012, Lang also edited *The Iron Mountain Review* for twenty years and coordinated the Emory & Henry College Literary Festival for twenty-five years.

Kevin D. LeMaster is currently an avid student of poetry. His poetry has been included in *Red Fez, Jellyfish Review, The Lakes, Counterpunch*, and others, including local newspapers. He has served as poetry editor for *Silhouette* magazine and prose editor for *Twizted Tungz*. He currently resides in Northern Kentucky with his wife, children, and grandchild.

Luke Marinac received his MFA from Bowling Green State University in 2017. He served as the book reviews editor for the *Mid- American Review*, and his poems have previously appeared or are forthcoming in the *North American Review*, the *Pittsburgh Poetry Review*, and *Stirring*, among others.

Micah McCrary is a contributor to the *Los Angeles Review of Books*. His essays, reviews, and translations have appeared in *Essay Daily, Assay: A Journal of Nonfiction Studies, Brevity, Third Coast*, and *Midwestern Gothic*, among other publications. He co-edits *con•text*, is Assistant Editor at *Hotel Amerika*, and a doctoral student in English at Ohio University. He holds an MFA in Nonfiction from Columbia College Chicago.

Rebecca Schamore lives in Kingsport, Tennessee, where she teaches writing to tenth and eleventh graders at the local high school. She holds an MA in French from Vanderbilt University and is currently working on an MFA in Creative Nonfiction through Spalding University in her hometown of Louisville, Kentucky.

Noel Smith spent several years in Leslie County, Kentucky, as a social worker for the Frontier Nursing Service in the 1950s and 1960s, sometimes visiting her clients on horseback. A native New Yorker, she returned home where she taught elementary school. Her book *The Well String* includes narrative poems about the people she knew while in Kentucky. She now lives in the lower Hudson Valley of New York.

Larry D. Thacker's poetry and prose can be found in or is forthcoming in journals such as *Still, The Southern Poetry Anthology: Tennessee, Broad River Review, Rappahannock Review,* and *Delaware Poetry Review*. He is the author of *Mountain Mysteries: The Mystic Traditions of Appalachia*, the poetry chapbooks *Voice Hunting* and *Memory Train*, and the forthcoming collection, *Drifting in Awe*. He is taking his poetry/fiction MFA from West Virginia Wesleyan College.

C. Williams's fiction has appeared in *The Louisville Review* and *Appalachian Heritage*. When not writing, she works as a production designer for sets in film, television, and commercials. She lives on the eastside of Nashville, the best neighborhood in the known world.

T.M. Williams is the 2011 recipient of the Jean Ritchie Fellowship in Appalachian Writing. Her work has appeared in *Still: The Journal, Waxing & Waning*, and various *Motif* anthologies. A native of McRoberts, Kentucky, she currently lives in Nashville, where she writes fiction and songs.

A descendant of mountain people who moved to work in the mills that once flourished in the Virginia Piedmont, **Annie Woodford** now lives and teaches community college English in Roanoke, Virginia. Her poetry has appeared or is forthcoming in *The Chattahoochee Review, Bluestem, Tar River Poetry, Tinderbox Poetry Journal, Appalachian Journal*, and *Prairie Schooner*, among others.

William Kelley Woolfitt is the author of two books of poetry, *Beauty Strip* (Texas Review Press, 2014) and *Charles of the Desert* (Paraclete Press, 2016). His writings have appeared in *The Threepenny Review, Cincinnati Review, Michigan Quarterly Review,* and *Radar Poetry*. He teaches at Lee University in Cleveland, Tennessee.